Keeping MUM

Keeping MUM

SECRETS of happy PARENTING and other lies

BRONWYN DONAGHY

HarperCollins*Publishers*

HarperCollins*Publishers*

First published in Australia in 1997
by HarperCollins*Publishers* Pty Limited
ACN 009 913 517
A member of the HarperCollins*Publishers* (Australia) Pty Limited Group

HarperCollins*Publishers*
25 Ryde Road, Pymble, Sydney NSW 2073, Australia
31 View Road, Glenfield, Auckland 10, New Zealand
77–85 Fulham Palace Road, London W6 8JB, United Kingdom
Hazelton Lanes, 55 Avenue Road, Suite 2900, Toronto, Ontario M5R 3L2
and 1995 Markham Road, Scarborough, Ontario M1B 5M8, Canada
10 East 53rd Street, New York NY 10032, USA

The National Library of Australia Cataloguing-in-Publication data:

Donaghy, Bronwyn, 1948– .
Keeping mum: secrets of happy parenting and other lies
ISBN 0 7322 5778 6.
1. Parenting – Humor. 2. Parenting – Anecdotes
I. Title.
649.1

Printed in Australia by Griffin Paperbacks
9 8 7 6 5 4 3 2 1

99 98 97

DEDICATION

To Francis, Aidan, Anna, Liam and my own, wonderful Mum, Nancy.

Thankyou for your inspiration, love and laughter.

Of course, any resemblance between you and the people in these pages is purely coincidental!

ACKNOWLEDGEMENT

Most of the essays published in this book have appeared in similar form in Sydney's Child, Melbourne's Child *(the 'Storming Around' column),* The Sydney Morning Herald, Family Circle *and* Australia's Parents *magazine.*

Frances Storm is the pen name used by Bronwyn Donaghy when writing for Sydney's Child.

CONTENTS

PERFECT PARENTS STOP READING NOW

A man rang a radio talkback show the other day and said he was the proud father of four grown children. One had become a lawyer, one a teacher and two were doctors. He and his wife had raised them with common sense, love, discipline and justice and as a result the children were living happy, productive and fulfilled lives. If more parents followed this sensible and compassionate approach to bringing up children, he said, the coming generation would be a better one.

This book is not for him.

A female politician was reported in a women's magazine as saying that most mothers were stimulated by child rearing. She said that watching their girls and boys grow up was reward enough for the women who put their careers, hopes and dreams on hold while they uncomplainingly bore the babies, brought up their children, maintained their homes and found part-time jobs which enabled them to continue to be chauffeurs, marketers, counsellors, chefs, chauffeurs, educators, nurses, diplomats, chauffeurs, fashion coordinators, travel consultants, chauffeurs, investment advisors, peacemakers and by the way, chauffeurs, throughout the arduous but stimulating years during which they were raising their families.

This book is not for her.

If the women she described actually existed it would be for them. But they don't.

This book is definitely not for Everyone Else's Parents. In fact, it's because of them that ordinary mothers and fathers need books like this.

In other words, this book is about the rest of us!

This book is about all those mums and dads who have never seen a child of theirs leap up from reading a story in order to look up an unknown word in a dictionary.

This book is for the chefs who are tired of cooking meals which inspire the nightly comment: 'Why can't we have take-away?'; for the marketers with bruised and bleeding ankles who watch their lives wheeling past them every time they push a supermarket trolley. It's for the counsellors who remember what they should have told their kids to do the day after the note comes home; the consultants whom nobody consults, the doctors and nurses whose progeny have caught every virus known to child; the educators whose memory of algebra stops with 'let the unknown distance be *x*' and whose mastery of modern education technology is limited to finding the Enter key.

It's for diplomats who are sick of dipping; who have sometimes even said: 'Hit him back!' It's for chauffeurs who pray for rain or secretly root for the other team so that sooner or later, maybe just one day of the week, they won't have to chauffe.

This book is for all the women who have come out, who have actually acknowledged to each other in shock, relief and disbelief that THEIR kids do that too.

This book is for parents who peel apples, cut off crusts, put the toothpaste on their children's brushes and squirm with guilt when asked by a five-year-old headed for a career in futures trading: 'Do I have to use my own money?'

This book is for the mother who guided her baby's thumb into his mouth, for the woman who never bought brown bread, for the parents whose backs are permanently racked from bending over to pick up their children's toys and dirty underwear, for the father who refused to buy his four-year-old son a bride doll even though he knew it was a sexist decision.

This book is for parents who would not choose the adjective 'stimulating' when describing the way they feel about bringing up their families. Not early on Saturdays when they drag themselves out to soccer and netball, not on Monday nights when they are still matching up socks at midnight, not at three a.m. any day when Something is crawling out of the electricity socket.

This book is for the mother whose baby didn't sleep through the night until he was seven and for the father who bought his daughter a mouth organ when she asked if she could study at the Conservatorium.

It's for every woman who has said on the telephone: 'I suppose I should hang up and find out what they're doing'. And didn't.

Most parents are so busy washing, cooking and driving, sandwiching earning a living between cutting sandwiches, getting their children to gymnastics and swimming lessons, reading stories, buying food, throwing birthday parties, scoring, sorting out fights and sewing on badges, that they don't recognise quality time even when they fall into it. They just enjoy it when it happens, which is how it's meant to be.

Most parents eventually realise that they will never win, because even though they've been training for years, they still haven't learnt the rules. How can they, when with each new age and stage of their children's lives, the rules keep changing?

Mums and Dads of Australia, never forget that you are not alone. In fact it may surprise you to learn that some of us are doing even more badly than you.

After all, none of you gave birth to the Storm children.

INTRODUCING THE STORM CHILDREN: Turbulence, Serenity and Rash

The first big mistake I made as a parent was during the birth of my eldest child, Turbulence. Foolishly I let them cut the umbilical cord.

So worried about coming into the world was Turbulence that he refused to budge from his warm and peaceful place beneath my billowing smock; eventually — not soon enough — he had to be persuaded to leave by unnatural and not particularly pleasant means. Three weeks after his due date he was dragged, kicking and screaming, into the twentieth century.

Turbulence has never really forgiven me for letting the doctor make the unkind cut which put an end to his chances of remaining in that place where it was quiet and peaceful, where there wasn't enough room for the place to get untidy, where the routine never changed and where all the activity centred solely on him.

I tried to compensate for this by sticking to a rigid routine involving little else but breast, bed and burping. I attempted to convince him he was still inside by swaddling him tightly in a bunny rug for the first six months of his life; this made his head look large and contributed to his wide-eyed and somewhat startled expression, but it paid dividends as it also kept the rather ghastly things that were going on at his business end under control.

Turbulence was so mature by the time he was born that he was a reasonably quiet infant. It wasn't until he was about a year old that he began to notice that he was being forced to live in a messy world where adaptability is essential to survival. He's been worried about everything ever since and we have spent his lifetime pitching on the churning waves of his emotions.

Serenity was late too, no doubt because she couldn't find something at the last minute, but she arrived calmly and her birth performance was faultless as would be all her public performances in the future. She didn't notice the mess she had made, falling instantly back to sleep in her father's arms. My mistake here was that I didn't wake her up and make her roll up the umbilical cord and neatly put it away, thereby instilling good training from an early age. She has never rolled up or put away anything since. Nor has this worried her in the slightest.

Rash battered his way out when nobody was expecting him, couldn't find time for a sleep for the next few days because he was so busy roaring, being sick and developing his allergies and if someone had handed him the scissors, would have happily cut the umbilical cord himself.

My mistake was that I wouldn't let him. Did I think he was a baby or something? Everyone Else's Mother would have let him. From Day One I failed him.

Like most people, I became a parent by accident.

This doesn't mean that Turbulence was unplanned; it means that although I wanted a baby, I was unprepared for the fact that this made me a mother.

When you become a parent you are suddenly responsible for somebody else. You are in charge of another life. Everything you do, from the way you chew, to the place you keep your toilet cleaner, may have a long-term effect on another human life.

I had imagined having children. I had a mental picture of a glossy-haired group with straight side partings and straighter teeth. In the framed photo in my mind we were sharing a little joke before we all went inside to harmonise around the pianola.

I still think about that sometimes, usually on the nights Rash tortures us with trumpet practice.

I knew I would love my children and I do, so much and so unreasonably that sometimes the intensity, the anxiety and the inevitable guilt that comes with mother-love twists and squeezes my heart until it feels like a spin-dried jumper which I should have hand-washed and dried flat, out of the sunlight.

But like most novice parents I had imagined loving them would be enough. Love would get me through.

It's not. It doesn't. You need a lot of other tools as well. Like patience, for example, and wisdom and understanding, none of which are available in a boxed set from the big chain stores. You need mental agility so that you can remember twenty things every minute, ranging from who is sad today and why, to how many eggs are left in the fridge and who needs permission notes signed; you need the physical stamina to remain awake for long periods of time, carry cumbersome bags, push large loads and keep your mouth clamped shut when a scream wants to force its way out at inappropriate times.

Above all you need time, a precious commodity which is in tragically short supply all over the western world.

I had never contemplated the pressures of parenthood. The pain. The paranoia. Above all, the permanence. I had never planned to be burdened with such an awesome responsibility, never contemplated such total commitment.

Who does? Who could? Who would want to? Imagine how the birth rate would plummet if we all knew what lay ahead.

Only when I had children of my own did I realise my mother had not only looked after my health, safety, education and pillow slips for the first third of my life — she had been checking that my sisters and I had cleaned our teeth, remembered handkerchiefs, worn warm singlets and eaten apples every day, seven days a week, fifty-two weeks a year, for more than thirty years. Could I ever match her performance? Would I ever learn all the rules?

Most importantly, would I eventually be as gracious as she was in defeat? Because of course she realised years ago that despite the hankies and the apples and the singlets, or perhaps because of them, she couldn't win. She grasped early the single principle that applies to parenting — that mothers and fathers can't come out on top. If children achieve anything at all, whether it's success, happiness or hitting the pot first go, it's their triumph. If they fail, if anything goes wrong with their lives at all, it's their parents' fault.

She knew but like previous generations of mothers and fathers, she kept the secret. She stayed Mum.

And yet, my mother was pretty good at parenting. She did the best thing parents can do for their child. She convinced me that I was a very special and important person.

Then my children arrived and set out to prove that she was wrong.

Part 1

SAYONARA Self-esteem

Research has been assuring us loudly for years that physically, mentally and emotionally, children learn more during their infancy than they do for the rest of their lifetime.

What research keeps quiet is that when a woman reaches the state of maternity, she almost immediately begins the backward slide that results from reproduction. No matter how highly qualified she may be in her professional life, when it comes to motherhood, a woman finds herself untrained, unlicensed, unstable and unable to sleep – in other words, very poorly equipped to cobble together a whole new range of life's richest experiences, from pooh to pre-school. Full-time fathers find themselves in the same situation; roof men (the ones who go out every day to keep something over our heads) are more likely to retain some shreds of their self-esteem – at least until the weekend.

So as a parent, you're just a beginner? That may cover you for the first baby but what's the excuse when you're up to number two, three or even four? Nobody's going to believe that you 'simply forgot' about toilet training.

THE Longest DAY

You can always tell when it's nearly Mother's Day. At least once every twenty-four hours someone will howl: 'Oh MUM, you always spoil EVERYTHING!'

Mother's Day is the longest day of the year. Worse than birthdays. Worse than Easter. Worse even than Christmas, in the shops, on the roads and all through the tense and emotional hours that precede the main event.

Weeks before the day, smiling young pretenders with even teeth, sleep-satisfied eyes and hair as smooth as cellophane begin to slide on to television screens across the nation, stroking refrigerators and microwaves, cuddling cake mixers and four-door family sedans, flogging all those gifts that any four-year-old may be considering.

At home the abuse begins. Suddenly I'm in trouble for bringing clean underwear into their rooms, for searching for dirty washing, for changing their beds without once asking their permission to do so. Doors are slammed in my face; fumbling under beds for smelly socks, my fingers come into unwilling contact with glue-damp curly cards, raining glitter, and paddle pop constructions which snap and keel over at my tentative touch. As I drop the soccer boots onto a pile of plastic bags in Turbulence's cupboard, my stomach contracts at the sound of a ceramic autumn leaf, with my name on it, shattering into a thousand orange pieces.

On the eve of the Longest Day, I am an outcast. Every room seethes with secrets and as I drag the vacuum cleaner from door to door the cry goes up: 'Keep out! Keep away! Don't come in YET!'

'Whistle,' suggests Turbulence, 'so we know when you are hanging around.' I contemplate buying a bell and hanging it around my neck or bellowing 'unclean' as I tramp through the hall.

The big day dawns. I stumble out of bed to change the baby, then sneak back to doze until my nose is teased awake by the smell of burning toast. A kettle and the infant are screaming in the distance and my eyelids scrape across my pupils in time with the sound of an unseen knife blade removing burnt bits in the kitchen. Inevitably the crashing of shattered glass and the cries come together: 'I TOLD you that would happen!'

The breakfast tray arrives. Very thin pieces of darkly tinted cardboard are served with a perfectly round, rock-hard egg yolk. They have rescued enough jam to place a glob of it in the dear little crystal bowl where I keep my engagement ring when I'm not wearing it. I stifle a scream. I'm not wearing it.

Running my tongue over furry teeth, I help the presents out of a year's supply of sticky tape and the pretty paper I've been storing for emergencies. Two clothes pegs with rolling eyes and fur fabric eyebrows. A pink and red mat woven from strips of paper. My fifth floral picture frame. Talc. Chocolates. A set of barbecue tools the Good Husband has needed for ages. Their eyes never leave my face as I quiver with enthusiasm and delight. I cheer myself with the thought that I only have to do this once a year. Serenity drops her claggy card into the jam. There are tears. They won't be the last.

When they've gone, I slip into the shower so they can make my bed. I return to find they haven't. Gathering up the sea of paper and ribbons, I tidy the bedroom, change the baby again, put a load of washing into the machine, take a deep breath and step into the holocaust which was once a simple suburban kitchen.

The children have all gone next door to tell Everyone Else's Parents how happy they've made me. Everyone Else's Mum loves Mother's Day. She's unbelievably excited about her new iron. She wears her glittering light globe earrings all day long. I know this because her daughter, Nikky, comes in to watch me clean. She perches on a stool which stands in a sea of spilled milk and tells me how much her mother loved having a bowl of

Smarties for breakfast and how willingly she shared them. Nikky's gaze falls carelessly but frequently upon my choccies.

'You'd better go home and help her or she'll get cross,' I say, through gritted teeth.

'It's okay,' says Nikky. 'My mother is NEVER cross.'

I stack dishes, wipe benches, close doors and dispose of mountains of black crumbs and eggshells.

The children burst in. 'You're not washing up on MOTHER'S DAY?' I sit down quickly and grab a magazine. Of course not, I assure them guiltily. They nod sternly and disappear. They're not either.

The traffic on the way to Nanna's is impenetrable. She has lollies for the children and a cigar for GH. I get nothing. I'm her daughter, not her mother. I start peeling potatoes for the roast. My sister comes in to help. Beads of perspiration slide into the lines of exhaustion on her brow. She is wearing a necklace of blue macaroni.

Home at last, exhausted from an afternoon listening to the footy on Nanna's radio, turned up loud to drown the annoying noise made by mothers washing up, the father and his elder son sag in front of the footy on television. I bath the baby, iron the school uniforms, supervise Serenity's hair washing, slap strips of cheese on slabs of toast, fold up the clothes and cut tomorrow's lunches. Serenity has written HAPPY MO on the cake I bought but has been interrupted by her favourite television program about a motherless family whose children are ecstatically happy. Turbulence comes in looking hurt. 'You're not WORKING on Mother's Day?' He has brought his school shoes for me to clean.

Their father dashes out and returns with a huge bunch of anorexic chrysanthemums (you get more for your money if you buy at the end of the day). Like me, these are fading fast.

The children go to bed saturated with satisfaction. They've been wonderful and they know it. 'Poor Mum. Now you have to wait another 364 days.'

'I'm dying for a cup of tea,' I say, sinking into a chair.

'Thanks love,' says the Good Husband. 'That would be lovely.'

RISING Damp

It's springtime in suburbia. Children's temperatures are slipping back to normal, sickly white arms are sliding into the open, the air is filled with blossom and the house is full of sneezing.

It's the time of year when hormones gallop, thongs start appearing on the doorstep and for thousands of suffering, stressed-out parents everywhere, toilet training begins.

Even if she's put it off for so long that her child is on first name terms with his orthodontist, no self-respecting woman can justify leaving her toddler in nappies in the springtime.

It was easy to train my boys. When it came to pointing his most personal appendage at the porcelain, Turbulence was delighted to discover a practical use for the thing, after spending his first two years worrying about what it might be for.

I postponed training Rash for so long that eventually I was able to give him a book to read on the subject. One day I noticed he was trained. It's like that with third children.

But with Serenity, toilet training represented our first major clash.

Her reaction to being placed on our bright yellow commode was immediate and loud. Picking up her nappy, pins, and plastic pants, she pelted into her room and clambered up onto her change table, bellowing baby talk that translated roughly into the fact that she wanted decency to be folded and pinned safely once more between her legs.

During the rest of that first day, Turbulence used the potty several times, Froggy sat on it and so did Teddy and even Moth-Eaten, the Rabbit. Serenity worked off her sense of betrayal by unzipping the beanbag and freeing 2,000 pellets of polystyrene.

The next day I trapped her on the potty chair.

For the first hour of her imprisonment, Serenity did all her puzzles, heard fifteen stories, ate a bag of sultanas and ran over Turb's knuckles with the red racing car. She did not do a wee.

During the second hour, convinced that she must have something to offer, I sang, danced, clapped, cajoled, begged. My own boredom and exhaustion eventually gave her the victory. She sighed with relief as I freed her, and went to relieve herself behind her cot.

She then put on her rain boots and jumped on the damp patch.

We punished her by withdrawing sweet food. Faced with the choice between pot and goodies, Serenity chose a third alternative. She stopped weeing altogether.

Her normally plump, happy face developed a pinched expression as she wandered around the house, contracting every muscle in her small, determined body in the effort to shut off all her exit points. Her ears were closed to threat, command or plea. Her eyes were blind to the sight of the commode.

After eight days, Serenity had successfully cut herself down to two enormous wees a day, one early in the morning and another one in the late afternoon. This I tried desperately to anticipate by positioning her near the potty at W-hour and offering (by this time) lollies, chocolate biscuits and even a giant panda. I was always too late.

My hands broke out into a rash and my nerves became as threadbare as Moth-Eaten. I burned the dinners, forgot to bring in the washing and yelled at everyone. The house smelled like a sewer.

Turbulence broke first. He cried even more easily than usual and took his thumb and his pillow off to his bedroom where he had his favourite nightmare about The Thing That Comes out of the Electric Socket. His routine was ruined.

Desperate at six o'clock one sunny afternoon, knowing that Serenity had not relieved herself since ten-thirty that morning, I picked up the pot and began following her everywhere she went. A deep frown settled on her smooth brow. She wandered from room to room, out of the back door, into the garden. She pretended not to notice me as she went about her business, checking out the condition of the shrubs and having short, business-like discussions with passing ants. From the corner of her determined eyes she could see me hovering, yet she paid me no more attention than she would have given a black and cumbersome blowfly.

Turbulence followed us both, whimpering quietly, worrying away. For once I ignored him. Whatever this might be doing to his sensitive psyche would have to be dealt with at a later date. This time, I was going to win.

Suddenly Turbulence slipped and let out a howl. For a split second I turned towards him — and the battle was lost.

A tidal wave of urine splashed around our feet. At the last minute Serenity had grabbed Moth-Eaten, the Rabbit, and stuffed him between her legs to stop the flow; drops bounced off his synthetic chest and splattered the veranda. Serenity leaned casually against the commode and smiled at me.

We had to throw Moth-Eaten away. We put the potty chair in the garage and Serenity went back into nappies; her slow, serious smile returned.

Six weeks later, just as the final layer of skin was healing on my harrowed hands, Serenity came across the commode in the garage. She paused, pulled down her nappy, then sat down and used it.

Turbulence flung his pillow in the air and shouted: 'Now you can buy her a giant panda like you promised!'

I gave Serenity a resentful hug. 'So you decided to do it your way,' I murmured.

And as my daughter rested her fat, biro-covered cheek against mine, I knew for sure that she always would.

PLAYGROUP Addiction

Never admit to a cheerful, well-adjusted mother of trouble-free toddlers (yes, such a woman exists, I met her once in the natural yoghurt section of a supermarket — she was handing slices of apple to the children in her trolley and they were squealing with delight and gratitude) that you actually enjoy playgroup.

It's like confiding to a non-smoker how much you miss the bite of the drawback or telling a teetotaller how strong, sweet sherry used to be the only thing that got you through children's bath time.

And yet I have to admit that there was a time in my life when playgroup was the pinnacle of my week, when the chance to spend two hours with sympathetic women with imperfect children, who were treading the same cereal-sticky treadmill as me and mine, gave me the sort of boost I needed to help me face seven more days of ochre nappies, sleep deprivation and sick stains on my favourite blouse.

When the washing machine has sneezed all over the laundry and you've found eggy toast ground into the berber, when the baby has crawled into the folded nappies and the three-year-old has forsaken his magazine collage and glued your bras into the undies drawer instead, when there's no chance of freedom because your mother's making meringues for her keep-fit meeting and you can't afford to pay a baby-sitter . . . there's nothing like playgroup to restore a fragment of your sanity.

When Rash finally started pre-school I realised I had to leave playgroup after more than ten years. Although I no longer had a reason to go, I used to drive past the hall, or hang around the entrance, hoping they'd offer me a coffee or a snippet of gossip about the state of the finger paint; I was like a retired worker who had been longing for freedom but couldn't keep away from her former factory.

My young friend Bitsy looks at me in appalled disbelief when I tell her this; she thinks playgroups are boring and stressful. But Bitsy is younger than me; since becoming a mother she has had the advantage of postnatal depression support groups, self-esteem courses, baby books, specialist magazines and earnest counsellors with straight hair, scrubbed, sincere faces and flat-heeled shoes. None of these were around when Turbulence was born. Especially flat-heeled shoes.

Playgroup used to be my lifeline. Nobody there threw their eyes to the ceiling when orange juice was spilt on the playdough, nobody pursed their lips or looked irritated, in the way shop assistants and childless friends do, when biscuits were crumbled underfoot and glue was spread on chairs. Nobody's eyes glazed over when we described how many times the baby had cried between three and five a.m. and we didn't turn up our noses when discussing the contents of our babies' nappies.

When people arrived with biters and pinchers we passed the word around and kept our children at a safe distance but even then we sympathised with the parents. There, but for the grace of God, we murmured . . .

Perhaps Bitsy just hasn't found the right playgroup yet. Like getting a really comfortable pair of high heels, you sometimes have to try a few playgroups before you find one that fits you really well — that gives you a lift without cramping your style or pinching your self-esteem.

I was introduced to the idea of playgroup by a clinic sister who looked at me sternly through her glittering bifocals and told me that because Turbulence was an only child, he needed stimulation and some company brighter than mine.

Chastened, I wheeled him home and rang the number she had given me. I had never thought of Turbulence as an only child — just the only one we had at the time. I was guilt stricken at the thought that I had thrust this small ten-month-old boy unaccompanied into a childless world.

The following week we found ourselves standing uncertainly on the ramp outside a modern hall. Well — I was standing. Turbulence had yet to take his first step. Clutching my baby in my arms I was forced to leap from the concrete as three huge crewcut thugs on massive tricycles hurtled towards us, shrieking battle cries. An enormous multi-ringed fist clamped down upon my arm and the mother of the revolutionaries frogmarched me into the hall.

'I am Helga,' she boomed. 'Put ze boy on ze mat and I vill gif you your chobz.'

Turb sat like a stunned mushroom on a rug, hypnotised by the massive three- and four-year-olds on vehicles who roared around him. I was shown the card file system which listed my chobz for the day and how to do them. All being well, an overseer would tick my card before I was allowed to leave. Presumably if I failed to perform to military standards, Turb would be held as a hostage.

We escaped through a side door; I promised my son we would return when he could ride a three wheeler — or at least toddle to safety — and I could accurately slice an apple into thirty-eight pieces in twenty seconds flat.

'Do you have band or singing together?' I asked the leader of my next playgroup, a tall girl wearing a floating scarf. 'Aah, musical expression. Aah. Wonderful. Sooo good for them. Aah.' She smiled at me through heavy-lidded green eyes. 'No, we don't.'

At one end of the room, intense and sibilant and stroking cups of coffee with many-ringed fingers, were the parents. 'This is Tory and Snooty and Pip and Sludge and Toffee and Zoe,' she said airily 'and those . . .' she gestured vaguely to the other end of the room, 'are the . . . um . . . children.'

Her friends exhaled pleasantly in my direction but immediately returned to a discussion about the advanced intellects of their six matching five-year-olds. I placed Turbulence among their six matching three-year-olds who were tipping out all the puzzles into piles. A little later I left the women's group, which was discussing the tax dodges of their six matching husbands, to discover that the youngsters were playing with the tap in the toilet.

'Aah, water play, sooo good for them,' said Scarf but I decided Turb had access to quite enough taps at home. Back to the drawing board.

The best thing about my perfect playgroup when I finally found it was that while I mixed up the paint, a group of athletic one-year-olds took it in turns to wheel sixteen-month-old Turb around in his stroller. Three wheelers — and indeed, walking — were still very much in the future. The hall was so old that its single tap was too stiff for any of us to turn on without help.

But a playgroup doesn't depend for its success on aesthetic appeal. We had playdough and paint and dressing up and band, blocks and bouncing and singing silly songs. We had laughter and tears and temper tantrums and more laughter. Serenity was born into that playgroup; it was there she developed her love of craft and began her life-long destruction of state forests. Rash, when he eventually crashed his way out of my womb and into the group, loved the drums and the slippery dip and the kids who squealed and let him chase them, first on his fat knees, later on foot and eventually on the playgroup's plastic tractor.

My playgroup friends pretended not to notice the damp patch under Serenity when I told them how efficiently she had toilet trained herself. My playgroup friends sympathised while I told them about Turb's problems at Big School. My playgroup friends showed me how to get navy blue paint off Serenity's cream velvet smock and my playgroup friends carried Rash's front teeth for me while I ran, carrying him in my arms, to the nearest dental surgery, on the memorable playgroup day when he went over the handlebars of the new three-wheeler trike.

Poor Bitsy. I just hate to think that she might miss out on all that fun.

THE NANNA Factor

Turbulence was five years old when his grandmother disappointed him for the first and only time in his life. He discovered that she did not actually play rugby league for Parramatta.

'You mean she just WATCHES?' he asked incredulously. 'She spends all that time SITTING DOWN?'

We had to explain that his grandmother had not been spending her weekends tackling packs of panting hunks, wearing shiny shorts under her drip-dry slacks and endangering her beautifully preserved dentures.

Had he really imagined that every Sunday, she spent her time disturbing her permanent silver waves with head-hugging tackles, or racing over the touch line in her well-polished pumps?

'This is going to be embarrassing,' growled Turbulence. 'I was the only kid in the grade whose Nanna played league.'

Inevitably it was us, his deceiving parents, who bore the full force of his anger and disappointment. He forgave his Nanna as soon as he saw her again.

How could he not? Turbulence adores his grandmother because she gives him that special, totally undeserved respect that he believes is his right as the first grandchild — and because she has never yelled at him, blamed him for anything, interrupted him or made him feel guilty in his entire life.

She catches her breath as she watches him clear small shrubs with a single bound, she claps when he performs feats with his feet so wondrous you couldn't believe that his mother thought shoe marks on the wall mattered. She produces a spare hanky whenever he sniffs (and doesn't ask why he forgot his own), she cries tears of mirth when he cracks a joke (and never rolls her eyes), she is breathless with admiration when he creates technical masterpieces with Lego or Meccano (and never mentions mess). When he shows proof of academic brilliance, she is never surprised, when he is hungry she provides chocolate (and never suggests fruit) and when he hurts she instantly produces something sweet to take away the pain. In his entire life, my mother has never told Turb to eat an apple or put on a singlet!

How can a mother or father possibly compete with that?

Keeping up with their own parents is one of the most difficult challenges for the current generation of mothers and fathers. Our parents are old but they are interesting and enthusiastic about everything their grandchildren do; our children are young but they are interesting and enthusiastic about their nannas and pops. We're the ones in the middle, managing the families, earning the salaries and feeling about as boring as Brussels sprouts.

Grandparents today are such a mixed bunch. The grey-bunned variety who home-bake scones are outnumbered by the Sara Lee set. Nannas and grandads go to work; they drive snazzy cars and wear snazzier jeans. Those who retire travel Australia in campervans, go to bowls tournaments whenever you need them to baby-sit or jet out to exciting foreign places, bringing back funny pyjamas and T-shirts with rude slogans.

A lot of grandparents WEAR T-shirts with rude slogans.

They dance with their hips clamped together under green neon lights in clubs. They paint pictures at evening classes. They march in demonstrations and race in wheelchairs. They light fires, swim long distances, sail sleek yachts and hang up on talkback radio hosts.

Some get punk haircuts, some get divorced, a lot go back to university and do courses in Human Geography and Statistics, subjects in which you've always thought they were already expert.

They go to the football on Sundays and their middle-aged sons sometimes have to separate them in the stands.

But they don't actually PLAY.

Turbulence forgave his Nanna this one blot on her copybook because what she does and how she looks is not as important to him as the confidence he derives from knowing what a very special place he holds in her fuzzy cardigan-covered heart; he is secure in the knowledge that the mere thought of him brings a proud lump to the place where she ties her permanently drooping white polyester bow.

Serenity, however, who had the misfortune to be born female, second and entirely without tact, has no illusions about Nanna's increasing years and limited abilities.

No matter how smart Nanna is looking, nor how robust she may feel, Serenity, in her slow, serious way, never misses the chance to discuss her grandmother's inevitable deterioration.

'I decided it was time I looked like a grandmother,' said my mother gaily, when she finally allowed her hair to go from artificial Midnight Black to natural silver-white. 'You looked like a grandmother before,' said Serenity thoughtfully. 'Now you look like an old lady.'

Serenity chooses public places and family reunions to point out sympathetically that Nanna's hair is thinning alarmingly, that Nanna's toes are oddly buckled, that Nanna has lines and lumps where Serenity is smooth, that Nanna's hands look like the pictures in her atlas, that Nanna quivers in places where Serenity is firm. When Nanna dons her black cossie to get a better view of Turb riding the waves, Serenity bobs up and down beside her in the shallows and asks her if she knows her back wobbles. When they have a cuddle on the couch, Serenity sees nothing wrong with offering to count the wrinkles in Nanna's neck.

On chilly winter nights my mother lies awake on a sea of sheepskin guaranteeing sleep, worrying that with the onset of their joint maturity, her relationship with Turbulence might suffer and that her infallibility in his eyes might diminish. To guard against this she has learned by heart the names, ages and major hits of his favourite rock group.

Her concern is unwarranted. Turb's faith in his Nanna is as unwavering as their joint conviction that one day, Parramatta will win again — if not in Nanna's lifetime, at least in Turb's. My mother would do better to worry about the fact that Serenity has meanly passed on some harsh facts of her life to her little brother, who is less forgiving than Turbulence and absolutely mortified.

'You mean she just WATCHES?' howled Rash.

A SPORTING *Chance*

A large woman with Judith Durham hair, a grey tracksuit and a face like a trampoline, came and stood near me at the fence rail. She lit a cigarette and squinted through the smoke and late afternoon sun, nodding with approval as a small boy wearing shoulder shields crunched to the ground at our feet and disappeared under a pile of clamouring bodies.

I sucked in my breath and she looked at me mildly.

'They love it,' she said. 'Mine just can't tear hisself away.'

It occurred to me that it would have been dangerous for him to try.

By the time Turbulence had reached his tenth birthday he had already been wanting to play rugby league for two years. We finally gave in. After years of peer pressure during which we subjected him to as many sports as our friends and relatives thought were suitable, it seemed like a quaintly original idea to let him choose one for himself.

Peer pressure plays a big part in sport for children. Not their peers, ours. I was only just recovering from Turb's first weeks at school when it was made clear to me that if my son was old enough for an education, he was old enough for soccer.

I am from a family of sisters; we were brought up in a country town where the local idea of sport was leaping over cowpats and watching Wimbledon on the teev. We played no sport until we were at high school, where we discovered that what we shared apart from our parents was a complete absence of hand–eye coordination.

My Good Husband spent his childhood in an Irish village where the boys played soccer in the street with a ball that had been around since Brian Boru; he had even less experience of organised children's sport than I did.

We paid out for the registration fees, membership to an obscure sporting club with a teddy bear logo, studded boots, Eskimo-weight socks, planks of foam and rubber designed to protect Turb's tiny shins and optional — but essential — satin shorts. I quickly learned that in the world of sport, no self-respecting mother lets her child run on to a playing field in cotton!

Turbulence, who had always shown a preference for jigsaws over balls, danced around the paddock with a lot of other little boys, wearing gleaming shorts, gates on their legs and Crimplene shirts, provided by the club and washed weekly by the mothers in grey tracksuits who lined the oval in cheering hordes.

In one corner of the field, a small, skilled group of Scottish and Serbian boys tossed the ball from toe to toe and looked serious. As the weeks of the competition progressed, these little naturals, with their corkscrew legs and magnetised toes, steered the ball over the grass as if it was connected to their expensive boots with invisible wire. They were good.

You wouldn't have noticed that Turbulence was on the team.

On the colder mornings he wasn't.

As the soccer season progressed, a lot of the new boys got better and ran in the right direction. Some occasionally kicked a goal. A woman in a grey tracksuit, who was married to the South African team manager, bawled at the Limelighters throughout every game: 'Mork yaw mun!' but not even the Serbs knew what she meant.

Eventually they put Turb in goal, and he stayed there for the winter. He waved to us a lot and caught many colds. In six months he touched the ball twice. He had no mun to mork.

I should have learned my lesson from his swimming experience. I had only just passed in his last nappy as a chamois for the family car when peer pressure convinced me that we needed to give Turb swimming lessons. They weren't delivering babies underwater at that stage, but the trend to turn grass into liquid had begun and many of our friends had pools. On one occasion I had been forced to leap, fully dressed, into the kidney-shaped jewel in the crown of my friend's back yard, to drag Turbulence to safety. Moana had looked at me with reproach and pointed out that her own child had been doing laps before she knew her colours.

Turb was two at the time. We took him to a recommended swimming coach. An ex-Olympian in a grey tracksuit prised my money and my child from my arms and tossed him into his chlorinated nightmare, where a waiting Amazon with a wet ponytail and arms like doughnuts caught him.

For five days she towed Turbulence up and down the pool and for five days he screamed. Eventually she admitted he was too small and tossed him back.

'It's not the constant crying I mind,' she boomed as I wiped my own anguished tears from his sodden floaty, 'it's just the noise he makes while he's doing it.'

Through sheer determination and willpower (mine) Turb eventually became a good swimmer. Six years and a fortune in coaching fees and petrol later, he entered his first swimming carnival. He was the only eight-year-old in primary school who could swim 200 metres, all strokes.

In his age race, over a mere fifty metres, he swam so slowly that they announced recess before he got to the end of the pool. Finally, two teachers who wanted their tea and biscuits jumped in and towed him to safety. I approached with caution, smiled at them apologetically and then glued my eyeballs to Turb's.

'Well done, darling,' I hissed through gritted teeth. 'But don't you think you could have swum a little faster?'

Turbulence looked surprised. 'Of course,' he said. 'But I didn't want to get puffed.'

He refused to go in any other event as he realised it would cut into the time available for queueing at the canteen.

I never watched him during nine months of tennis lessons because I was sidetracked by a new baby. I just signed the cheques for the lightweight racquet, the shoes, the socks, the white clothing and countless coaching sessions. One day when I heard him tell his friend that 'deuce' was something you drank after a match, I decided to make the effort to go and check his progress.

As I pushed my pram towards the gathering of women in grey tracksuits beside the court, the coach called out to me with the innocent enthusiasm of the truly desperate: 'Hey! What a shame you didn't get here a bit sooner! He hit the ball today!'

Every time they fired the gun at Little Athletics, Turb was tying his own or someone else's shoelaces. He was really good at that. When he found out they weren't using tennis balls at cricket practice, he became nauseous at the crease.

He was getting good marks at school but it wasn't enough. Baseball jarred his hands. He was too short for basketball. But after years of swimming, he developed broad shoulders and his legs, while short, were sturdy. When he said he wanted to try league, we let him.

We paid the registration fees, joined a club whose logo was a horned beast with obvious nasal congestion, bought bigger boots with sharper studs, more Eskimo socks, more nylon shorts, a mouth guard and bandaids.

Mums are in the minority at league training. With just the one grey tracksuit at my side, I watched the boys tackle punching bags, tackle truck tyres, tackle each other. Small boys clawed at eyes and ankles and rolled in the dirt; big boys wheezed and panted, frowned, swore and sat on each other.

My fellow spectator removed her cigarette and opened her lungs.

'Giddup, Dagger, ya lidel frawd!' She took a breath and leaned forward: 'One of youse tickle 'im or somethink!' She replaced her cigarette and beamed at me. 'They love it,' she said.

When Turb trotted off the field he was red-faced but whole. He said he had a headache. We climbed into our car. The smell of his feet took my breath away.

'I think it's fair to tell you straight away that I don't want to do this any more,' he said.

I nodded. Was he hurt, I asked?

'No,' he replied thoughtfully. 'It's not because I'm hurt. It's because I'm GOING to be.'

I gunned the motor and headed straight for the shops. It was too late for his boots and socks but I was going to get my money back on my new grey tracksuit.

THE INCREDIBLE IMPORTANCE OF Shopping ALONE

I realised something strange was going on when I saw a shop assistant. She was right there, in the flesh, among the shelves, not busy, not on her way to a tea break, not in deeply serious conversation with a colleague. Incredibly, she seemed to be approaching me. Actually coming over. Wanting to talk. Perhaps, dared I hope, prepared to help me find what I needed?

Of course I was wrong.

'Excuse ME!' she shrieked, as I brought the stroller to a stop under a fan of disembodied legs in multi-coloured nylon.

'Look at this!' she shouted angrily, waving a large chocolate rabbit, dressed in a glittering red and silver suit which would have done Liberace proud. Well — partially dressed. Most of the bunny's tummy was missing. 'Your son destroyed this item of stock,' she hissed.

'He couldn't have done that,' I murmured. 'He's been with me in his stroller.'

'He did it,' she said grimly. 'He grabbed it off the shelf while you were pulling all those tracksuit tops off their hangers.'

I felt my face become hot. 'Well, can YOU explain why all the girls' size twelves are bigger than the fourteens?' I demanded, but she wasn't fazed.

'You'll have to pay for the rabbit,' she snarled.

I didn't want to pay $9.90 for an incomplete animal. I wanted to complain that they shouldn't keep chocolate treats at stroller level, that it wasn't fair of them to put edible rabbits within easy reach of toddlers who were bound to be tempted by their dairy milk tummies.

I didn't, of course. I paid up and took the bunny home to melt him down for cooking chocolate. It was my fault, after all. I was a grown-up, wasn't I? I knew the facts of life. There IS nothing FAIR about shopping in the company of children — and not only two-year-old children. Shopping with kids of any age should be banned by law. In an ideal world there would only ever be two of us down at the mall: me — and my list. Bliss!

Age two is bad but three is worse. How do you describe the horror of that moment in the fitting room, when you look down and see only your child's feet, as he lies on his back gazing curiously up at the fleshy delights of the unsuspecting person in the next cubicle?

What do you say at the delicatessen, when your son glances up at the pepperoni sausage hanging above the counter and says: 'Dad's got one of those, hasn't he Mum?'

Supermarkets aren't so serious. You can wedge toddlers into trolleys and stuff them with large, sticky silencers, although my friend Moana said only childbirth itself matched the pain of baby Natty's revenge — a large can of pears dropped from a trolley seat on to her sandalled toe. Even after they took the plaster off, she never shopped with a child again.

When they get older, small girls and boys become Grabbits. As most children over five refuse to risk public ridicule by holding their parents' hands, Grabbits are free to lunge out in all directions in search of the dubious delights the television has been offering them; never content to look, they always have to touch everything in sight.

And almost everything a Grabbit touches is holding up something else.

In newsagencies, horrible little Grabbit fingers are into every compartment at the counter, fingering the rolls of lollies, stroking the sherbet whistles, poking the jelly snakes. They have already removed all the matching envelopes from the cards and at least one of your children has asked you loudly why the lady wearing the rabbit's tail on the cover of that magazine is not wearing a singlet.

Or, for that matter, pants.

In the discount stores, they wind up the toys, take everything out of boxes, run their hands along lines of beige light shades, leave elbow indentations on piles of towels, fiddle with towers of rainbow lunch boxes and bounce the balls into the next aisle.

In the supermarkets they sweep sauce bottles to the floor when they're reaching for the Mars bars and insist on hanging around until the clean-up team arrives, just to make sure everyone in the store knows it was YOUR children who made the mess.

Personally, I prefer the embarrassment of sending staff running for the mop and bucket, to the humiliation of carting greedy Kenoivas through a supermarket.

Kenoivas are older than Grabbits. Aged from about eight, they believe it is necessary to spend the weekly housekeeping on everything that attracts their sharp and roving eyes.

'Kenoiva doughnut?' 'Kenoiva ice block?' 'Kenoiva bag of minties?' 'Kenoiva sticker book?'

'You don't have any stickers.'

'Well, kenoiv some stickers? To put in the sticker book?'

'Kenoiva locket like that one, cause everyone's got one except me?'

'Kenoiva bun to eat so I won't be bored while we're doing the shopping?'

Kenoivas operate on the single premise that if it's there, you should buy it.

'Kenoiva set of golf clubs to give Dad for his birthday?'

'Dad doesn't play golf.'

'He could learn.'

'Kenoi get one of those doormats?'

'We HAVE three doormats at home.'

'Yeah, but everyone's been walking all over those.'

Kenoivas graduate to Checkouts, who are usually eleven plus. Checkouts share your feelings about shopping with the family; they will do virtually anything to avoid being seen in public with you.

You have to plead with them to accompany you to the shops, but unfortunately, you need their feet or body for a fitting. Indeed, if it was possible, you would gladly leave the other bits of them at home. But Checkouts don't like to wait around.

'I'll just check out the record shop.'

'I'll just check out the milk bar.'

'While you're in here I'll just check out the latest issue at the newsagency.'

When you finally get them to try something on, they argue. The only clothes they like look like other people's cast-offs but cost more than your house extension. The only shoes that fit look like the vehicles councils use to mow public parks.

Some reprieve is offered when all your children are old enough for school. Alas, four times a year, the holidays descend — weeks and weeks of them.

It makes no difference how you choose to fill the chips and cordial days of summer . . . whether you throw the kids at a beach or arrange them limply around the pool, whether you import junior relatives with self-esteem problems to stay, or whether you visit far-flung friends with strained smiles, empty fridges and offspring who can't lie straight in bed . . . whatever you do and wherever you go, the shopping still has to be done.

Our last shopping excursion before school went back was for new uniforms. It was a long hard day, best forgotten.

'Mummy,' said Rash, as we unpacked the car, 'you still haven't told me why that lady on the magazine poster wasn't even wearing a singlet.'

We would both have preferred it if her tummy had been covered with a shiny red and silver suit!

SUFFER THE LITTLE Children

When the doctor rang the doorbell, Rash was propped up on pillows, pale as paste, his pink eyes closed against the pain.

So in what instant did the miracle occur? How is it that when the harassed GP walked through the front door, Rash was standing on the book shelf, wearing an orange lamp shade which clashed with his red cheeks, and aiming his twenty-two battery machine gun right at the poor man's head?

I hate that time of year, when temperatures go up, mucus runs down and germs go around in gangs, grabbing kids on their way home from soccer or music practice and slithering nastily into doctors' surgeries so that even brothers and sisters who are only there as spectators come out sporting runny eyes and whining like drills.

Fat jars of vitamin C tablets beckon from shop shelves but before you get to the checkout with them, the baby is sneezing and the big one is wheezing just from the effort of pushing the trolley.

Our children react very differently to illness.

Even in the middle of winter, with his mates crumpling like damp washing all around him, Rash refuses to give in to disease. What makes it worse is that he attracts every germ known to child and is allergic to our planet.

With clogged nostrils, watering eyes and a wheeze which is louder than the vacuum, he will race outside to try the trampoline. He can't swallow and his skin is as hot as the fire he accidentally lit in the lounge room, but he's Superman off the back of the couch, trailing a red cape and yellow phlegm and just missing the doctor who's saying he must be kept quiet for a day or two.

Rash heaves up any medication we give him and if we have been smart enough to put a bowl by his chair or bed, he is always sick out the other side. Rash's rashes mystify the medical profession. His cough blocks out the sound of low-flying aircraft. My cupboards are packed with equipment to bring back breath and I have trained myself to sleep while reading the *Muddle Headed Wombat* aloud to him at three a.m. Yet Rash will leap out of bed each morning, uncomplainingly throw gallons of medication down his blistered throat and race off to school without his jacket.

Inevitably, his teachers have us taped as THOSE sort of parents. Red-eyed, glands up, throat swollen, Rash is often sent to sick bay, but he climbs a few trees on the way and reports back to class after ten minutes.

Serenity is more prone to malfunctions in her body parts than to illness. Her toenails, for example, grow in. Her ears need grommets. Her eyesight is poor. During the long hours she spends cutting and pasting in her room, she has an unfortunate tendency to staple parts of herself to cardboard. On several occasions she has glued her thumb and fingers together.

When she does fall ill, Serenity suffers in silence. All day she lies miserably on the couch, staring at the television with huge, darkly shadowed eyes, eating nothing, drinking half a drop of water every hour from pursed, unhappy lips. She coughs harshly during the commercial breaks and her only pleasure comes from taking medicine. When you ask her how she feels, she closes her eyes in exhaustion, when you enquire for symptoms you cannot hear her faint replies. Almost inaudibly, she asks you to get her a bell, so that she can ring for service if she feels the need.

She worries us to death but I sometimes have the urge to boot her suffering little body right through the television screen.

Turbulence, our eldest child, is as strong as the proverbial ox and rarely gets ill. This is one of the many tragedies of his life as he would love the opportunity to be at home more often, taking refuge from the noisy and traumatic world which worries him so much. In truth, his tidy and organised nature would probably make him an ideal patient. While he never catches anything, he never gives up trying and in primary school he spent so much time in the sick bay that when they repainted it last year they consulted him about the colour scheme.

Winter forces difficult decisions on women . . . Should I make him go to school? Should I still go to work/lunch/canteen duty/shopping today or should I stay home and look after him? What if I am out and he has to be collected from school because he's worse? Should I call the doctor? Should I take her to the surgery? Is she infectious? Is he putting on an act? Will I change the sheets just for that damp patch or will I hold out in case he vomits again? Will I put a vaporiser in the room and risk all the wallpaper falling off tomorrow? What if I go to the doctor's and wait an hour and a half and then he says it's a virus and there's nothing he can do for her? Would our doctor be covered by insurance if I hit him? Will I give her that cough medicine that wakes her up and makes her want to sing all night?

In an ideal world, Rash would be as healthy as Turbulence and Turb could have all Serenity's malfunctions so that he could stay at home and enjoy them. In an ideal world, the children would not grin and bounce on the bed when the doctor walked wearily in.

I know I WILL get a full night's sleep again — just not soon — but I still hate feeling the cold and hearing the coughs and smelling the sick and watching the washing not drying on the line.

. . . And wondering whether her coughing is any worse than her singing.

COMING, Ready or Not!

If you make a cross with your forearms, slam them against your chest and grind your fingers into the tops of your shoulders, what do you get?

A five-year-old trying to fold his arms.

Rash cannot do it.

And this isn't his only problem.

'Miss Patience hid my scissors and the principal is keeping my ruler, PROBABLY because it's better than his,' he bellowed as he hurled himself through the front door. 'If this is big school why can't I use a PEN? You can't shoot anything with a pencil! It doesn't make a NOISE!

'And by the way,' he snarled, rubbing his short little arms disconsolately, 'STILL no smiley stamp!'

Something inside his brand new school bag smashed as it hit the slate tiles. My heart made the same noise as it broke for him.

After two months of school, Rash had not attained the ultimate: a red ink smiley stamp for being the first in the class to sit up straight with his legs crossed and his arms folded.

It's only when the initial excitement of starting school has worn off that the real difficulties, like arm folding and leg crossing, and high-speed eating, raise their sweaty little hands.

It seems only yesterday that the agony and the ecstasy of acquiring an education began in this family — can it be that the rapid passing of the children's school years means that somewhere along the way we've actually been enjoying ourselves?

It hardly seems likely, particularly when I think back to the day that our first child, Turbulence, started kindergarten. Turb received a stamp on his very first day of school; it was because he stopped crying at five minutes to three.

Turbulence was just four-and-a-half years old in that anguished February when I cut off his curls, bought him a grey shirt, some even greyer shorts and sent him, shocked and disillusioned despite hours of preparatory role play and all the right books, into the great big world. The colour of his face exactly matched his uniform.

How many years ago was it that a sodden, sobbing Turbulence was prised gently from my arms by a slender teacher with freckled arms and fluffy hair, who promised him a cuddle and lent some magic tissues, which were guaranteed to make tears disappear.

I hope she got her money back.

I remember how quickly I slipped into my daily habit of hovering around the toilet blocks, flattening myself against the brick wall, darting between the bubblers and straining for a glimpse of the assembled kindy kids, desperate to know whether Turbulence was still crying.

He always was.

Only Joshua Limerick's mother was worse off than me; she used to put on her flatties and run for her life with Joshua in hot pursuit.

Turbulence was bright, polite and frighteningly well-behaved, but far too worried about himself to become a successful student. Nobody warned me that knowing his alphabet and being able to work out the answer to twelve times twelve while he sat in solitary contentment on the toilet was not the same as coping with 144 pounding feet, 144 pushing, shoving bodies and 144 minutes a week of shrieking, snarling playground life. At least, not when you're only four.

Learning from my mistake, I kept both my younger children home until they were almost old enough to drive there themselves.

It paid off for Serenity. She floated through her first days of school so calmly and quietly that nobody noticed her at all. Someone sat on her in the bus and she failed to get a smiley stamp. This situation was quickly remedied of course, as the teachers soon realised she was the sort of student they fantasised about — bright, clean and quiet. She now has more gold stars than there are in heaven; if you put her merit certificates in a single stack it would be almost as high as Turb's pile of late notes.

More recently, on Rash's first day at school, he raced ahead of me through the gate, grabbed the hand of a plump teacher with straight hair and ivory arms and marched into his room without remembering to say goodbye.

I was left leaning against the bubbler wall with a vacant feeling in the area of my stretch marks which I first mistook for melancholy but eventually identified as relief.

Rash loves certain aspects of school, especially handball, canteen and Morning Fitness. He thought he might be a contender for a merit certificate for jumping on the spot for longer than anyone else in the class, but because he talked while he jumped, it wasn't to be.

Unfortunately his teachers keep interrupting the good stuff with lessons. He seems to spend most of these standing outside the principal's office, practising his arm folding.

Over on the other side of town, his cousin, Demanda is doing the same thing. My sister, Jade, an environmentally aware single parent with pacifist policies, has brought Demanda up to be a Free Spirit with a questioning mind. It is the sort of mind and spirit that stimulated Demanda, at the age of three, to interrogate people in the supermarket queue about the size and nature of their genitalia.

Demanda's first term of school introduced her to a totally foreign concept. It seemed that she was required to do whatever her patiently smiling teacher told her to do, even when no adequate explanation was provided.

Asked to close her colouring book, to join the class for singing on the mat, to remain in her seat, to fold her arms, to sit with her legs crossed or to stop talking, she demanded a reason. 'If it's a good one, I might do it,' she told her smiling teacher at the end of her first week.

My sister would prefer Demanda to be at a school more suited to free spirits . . . the kind where the taps run all day because the children haven't found a reason to turn them off, and where nobody forbids all the little Brookes and Skyes and Moonbeams from playing with knives and axes; the idea is that when they cut their fingers and toes off, they will learn by experience that sharp tools are dangerous.

But schools where Experience is the headmaster are dearer than ordinary schools where the children are taught by people, so Demanda is still at Upper Prickle Primary.

For very different reasons, children like Turbulence, Rash and Demanda are not the sort of pupils teachers welcome into their classrooms — and who can blame them? And yet we do — after all, it's the parents, not the teachers, who have to sit on the ends of the beds at night, soothing their troubled little souls and helping them calculate the number of weeks to the end of term.

Every morning Turbulence used to sit on the toilet for forty–five minutes in the hope that if he stayed there long enough, the school day might accidentally pass him by.

Rash has announced that he no longer has time to waste on the toilet.

On Turb's first day for taking 'news' we persuaded him out of showing the pillow he cried into at night. Instead he took a flower from his very own garden.

Rash, who had ridden his trike over the things growing in his very own garden, took his best sword and spent recess causing grievous bodily harm to the staff room roses.

Even though he was only singing in the chorus, Turbulence broke down halfway through his first kindy concert. The teacher playing the piano didn't even move her freckled fingers from the keyboard. 'Mrs Storm,' she said sweetly, swaying backwards towards the microphone, 'would you mind taking Turbulence off the stage so we can hear the other children singing? He's the tree howling in the fourth row.'

Rash only knew the words of Bon Jovi releases and offered to sing *Bad Medicine* at the school assembly. He accompanied himself on his toy guitar and for his finale, turned it into a rifle and shot the principal.

In Turb's fourth week he got into a fight because he told some big boys that it was against school rules for them to play in the kindergarten quadrangle.

On Rash's fourth day he got into a fight by attacking some roughnecks who were trying to beat up a little boy who cried.

'Luckily I'm tough,' he said. 'They were at least six, and they were tough AND . . .' he narrowed his eyes knowingly, 'they were GIRLS!'

Speaking of girls, my sister tells me that Demanda, like Rash, has spent a great deal of first term standing outside the classroom with her hands on her head. She's been asking for a reason why, but the smiling teacher won't give her one.

'One of them will become empowered soon,' said my sister. 'It will depend on who has the strongest spirit.'

My money's on Demanda.

These days, Turbulence endures school simply because it has become part of his routine and to Turb, Routine is Life. Serenity does her best at school and is happy as long as I pretend I don't notice how far above her knees she hitches up her uniform, and providing I let her wear men's white golf socks which she rolls down so that both her ankles appear to have been broken. Dressing like her peers is necessary if she wants to keep the affection of her friends, which is more important to her than education.

Miraculously, at the end of third term, Rash finally crashed through the school gate with his red stamped fist raised in a victory salute.

'You did it!' I yelped, swallowing the sob of relief which welled in my throat. 'You folded your arms!'

'No,' he said, joyfully, 'I got it because everyone else in the class has been stamped already and they always save the best till lucky lucky last!'

PREFERABLY NOT AN Octopus

Her fingertips were covered with tiny pinpricks of blood. White claggy globs oozed from under her nails and the unused bits of some unseen roll of sticky tape clung to her wrists. Tearing my gaze from the woman's tortured hands I looked into her wild eyes and knew immediately what she had been doing.

'Finished making Dumpling's costume?' I asked sympathetically. 'Is he in the class play?'

'It's for Cubs,' she croaked, plucking some staples out of her hair. 'They're having a 'come as your favourite animal' theme for their break-up meeting. Dumpling wants to go as a dinosaur.'

There was a silence as I tried to think of something sympathetic to say.

I couldn't.

'I can't work out a way to make it bend,' she continued bleakly. 'He'll have to stand up all night. And it's pretty dark inside the costume. He'll be tired and lonely in there. The tail keeps getting caught in doorways.

'I just couldn't talk him out of it.'

'Never mind,' I said at last. 'At least he didn't want to be an octopus.'

In households all over the country, as parents gather their strength for another big burst of costume creation, they are all longing for that wonderful moment when the year finally pulls the curtain on the dying snarls of strangled cellophane and crushed crepe paper.

For most of us the costume party starts early, with the Easter bonnet parades (no glue has yet been invented which will successfully stick cardboard and cotton wool to an ice cream container), followed by Commonwealth Day concerts, mid-year ballet and tap shows, musical eisteddfods, Cub and Brownie theme nights, fancy dress parties (do the parents who put these on ENJOY being despised and derided by their peers?), book week character parades and Education Week plays.

Just as we begin to enjoy the lull between spring and Christmas, commercial interests raise Halloween's orthodontically unattractive head and we have to start ransacking the linen cupboard for old sheets and wrestling with witches' hats. Finally we're all faced with end of year everything, most of which will require some sort of costume, at best a tea towel and a halo, at worst, the dreadful prospect of a child coming home with the joyful announcement that he has been selected as one of the six white boomers.

Our first son, Turbulence, never wanted to get dressed up in a fancy costume at school. In fact, he didn't want to go to school on the special occasions . . . well, Turbulence never wanted to go to school at all. But he found dress-up days particularly distasteful, because everybody became so excitable and noisy (especially the teachers) and lunch was at the wrong time and bits of his costume always fell off.

This was because having been convinced that he would feel left out if he didn't wear a costume, Turbulence always chose exceptionally difficult things to be.

Every year his primary school held a fund-raising walkathon in the adjacent reserve and in an effort to draw a crowd of barracking parents (you don't get a lot of adrenalin from standing in huddles watching 400 children walk around and around a circular track for three hours) the teachers introduced a different theme each year and asked the walkers to dress accordingly.

There were two problems with this idea. First, the walkathons took place in mid-winter, always an effective handicap to any type of dressing up. There's something about a cardigan over a grass skirt which kills the tropical effect. Second, even a sport as simple as walking requires a certain amount of dexterity which makes some costumes impractical.

'You have to get dressed up as SOMETHING,' I told Turbulence. 'Use your imagination. You have a wonderful imagination.' (After all, hadn't he spent years imagining the potential accidents which might do him harm?) 'Anything will do,' I pleaded. 'Anything.'

'If I have to, I'll be an octopus,' he said at last.

'Okay, you don't HAVE to dress up,' I said quickly.

'I want to be an octopus.'

'Anything but an octopus,' I said. 'Preferably not an octopus.'

Turbulence competed in the walkathon as an octopus. He wore a green tracksuit, a green knitted balaclava and four extra legs made from green tights stuffed with paper, one of which had dropped off before he even began the second circuit.

As he made his tearful, told-you-so way around the track, sympathetic mothers kept dashing forward, retrieving legs and bringing them to me with bright, painful smiles.

The same women had dressed their children in sensible jeans and given them a scarf and an eye patch, or pinned capes on their son's backs, and handed them cardboard party masks. Their daughters were mostly in mobcaps, apart from a few wand-wielding fairies with track pants under their tutus.

Years earlier Turbulence missed out on a speaking part in the nativity play but was allowed to choose between being a shepherd or one of the animals.

'A shepherd would be good,' I said hopefully. 'You could wear a tea towel on your head and look joyful.'

The tea towel was too simple and looking joyful was beyond his capabilities.

'I think I'll be a camel,' he said.

'Anything but a camel,' I replied. 'Anything.'

Turbulence went in the Year Two Nativity as a camel. His hump started to slide in the second scene and ended up tied to his tummy instead of his back. One of his hand-stitched brown velour ears fell off and hung from his chin.

The frankincense and myrrh spilled out of the tupperware pots and ran down his legs. He had to carry all the gifts because the wise men were sharing him — no other mother had been silly enough to let her child be a camel.

Rash doesn't mind dressing up as long as the outfit includes a weapon. The teachers hadn't realised the amount of damage you can do with a halo.

Unlike Turbulence and many other boys, girls are willing to dress up as almost anything, from giggling tramps with their teeth blacked out, to fairy princesses in gowns so gorgeously jewelled that you can't even see where their mothers' fingers have bled on them.

Serenity is no exception, but although she has been chosen frequently for major roles, the costumes she has been required to wear have been simple and easy. In fact the hardest costume I ever had to make for her was the one occasion when she missed out on a speaking part — she was the refrigerator in the Healthy Life Revue. We made her a lovely box to wear but her arms were too short to open her door and people kept knocking off her magnets.

On almost every other occasion she has been able to wear The Suit. This invaluable piece of parenting equipment is a short green taffeta tunic with a plunging neck and a ragged hemline, which incredibly, my career-conscious kid sister once wore to an office costume party. I have sometimes wondered whether it was this garment or her honours degree which helped her up on to the ladder to the glass ceiling. These days, worn over green P.E. shorts or tights, and occasionally tarted up with a bit of red crepe, it can be adapted as a costume for an elf, a fairy, a goblin, Peter Pan, Robin Hood, a sea sprite or even a green vegetable. Serenity once wore it to a Brownie concert when she was a Germ.

It was even simpler the year she was Mary. All I had to do was wash my blue tablecloth. But other mothers were not so lucky. Sadly, when sewing machines have been humming and staplers clack, clack, clacking long into the night, tempers begin to fray and competition comes creeping in. Which I suppose is why on the day of Serenity's play, one jealous mother, whose daughter missed out on the nativity but was chosen for the Healthy Life Revue, suggested to me that deals might have been done. She hinted that bribes (a donation to the library? a night of passion with the deputy principal?) had been exchanged for favours.

It wasn't so much the lead role that led to her uncharitable thoughts. It was the simplicity of Serenity's costume. I realised this because the woman was carrying a large white cardboard carton, trimmed in aluminium foil, with a door cut in the front and arm holes in the sides.

I knew for sure that her little Hope was this year's refrigerator.

'Be thankful,' I said. 'At least she's not a camel.'

OTHER KIDS' Mothers

She was tall and the parallel curves of her perfect silver streaks shone like a newly Ajaxed kitchen sink. Her clothes were in tones of rich gold and russet and her earrings were colour coordinated with her shoes. Her hemline was as straight as a slide rule.

As she descended the steps, hips undulating gently beneath folds of Country Road, I would not have been surprised to hear violins softly playing.

But this was not a Hollywood movie and this woman was not a film star. We were at the school gate and this was merely Another Kid's Mother, helping her son carry in a recyclable carton of freshly home-baked slice for cake day.

I sighed as I stretched my tired eyes towards the disappearing figure of my youngest child (carrying his Cheap-Mart lamingtons in a plastic ice cream container without help from me) and waited dutifully to see if he was going to grant me a final wave, or whether, like most mornings, I had left his mind the moment he had left my care.

Already my armpits were squeezing unsavoury damp drops onto my T-shirt which, at the spot where my stomach caresses the kitchen bench, already bore the familiar stain of blended breakfast and sandwich ingredients. The crutch of my shorts had slipped to the area of my knees. The synthetic uppers of my shoes had begun to crack.

I wasn't wearing earrings.

'Going to work?' I asked the Other Kid's Mother as she came back through the gate. I spoke in the slightly disapproving tones of a Mother Who Stays Home.

'It's my day off,' she said, exuding something expensive in my direction. 'I'm going home to hang out a load of washing and then it's tennis.'

The thought of this Meryl Streep lookalike hanging out washing depressed me even further. This was not a woman who lugged plastic baskets up to cliff-embedded clotheslines and wrestled with copulating towels. This mother would have a squeak-free clothes trolley and a flat back yard; the lines on her Hills Hoist would always be taut and I knew without having to ask that she would always have enough pegs.

I didn't even know her name but the truth was that I knew this woman's life as well as my own.

She had almost certainly stopped sensibly at two children. Her home was large and airy, free of the clutter of crippled car tracks, balding rugs and chipped pine furniture. She would have a pool and a vast family room whose floor shone even on Monday mornings.

Her handy little job would leave her two or three free days for tennis and shopping. Her husband worked long hours in the city but always managed to get time off for Education Day when he came to school with the video camera he had picked up on their last overseas trip.

Her children would do gym, ballet and cricket; if she had girls they would play piano; her boys would have saxophones or electric guitars.

From their necks to their knickers and especially on their long, slim feet, her children would be permanently clad in brand name apparel and of course, they would be allowed to do everything my children were not.

I sighed again, checked to see whether Serenity was racing back to me because she had forgotten her bus money/homework/lunch, then stomped off homeward to scrape caramel from the impractical hairs of my family room carpet which was crying out for a clean.

But as I rounded a corner, the unforgettably urgent cry of a baby in distress met my ears and on the footpath I saw a young woman floundering beneath a load of tiny humanity. Her stroller had tipped backwards, as strollers loaded with nappy bags and shopping invariably do. The baby's feet were kicking frantically above its head and it was squealing in shock; a toddler with legs so short they seemed attached to his nappy, bellowed at her ankles and twisted the zig zagging hem of her faded dress into lumps as he screamed to be lifted up into safety.

The air around them was full of misery.

I didn't even know this woman's name but I knew her life as well as my own.

She was surviving on five broken hours of sleep a night, her nappy bucket was never empty and her family room, if she had one at all, was jammed with high chairs, toys, sticky messes and a bouncer which grabbed her ankles whenever she staggered through with a load of washing.

She too was Another Kid's Mother, I thought, as I helped her reassemble her squawking children.

And I took myself into my nice cool house which was almost certainly cleaner and quieter than hers would be and sipped an uninterrupted cup of coffee feeling almost cheerful.

The next day as I watched Mrs Silver Streaks slide into the eagerly awaiting grey leather curves of a low-slung sedan at the school curb, with a pile of washed (and ironed!) soccer shirts on the back seat, I managed to remain almost philosophical. Then, on my way home someone called out to me from the big white house on the corner. I blinked. It was the crumpled girl from the day before, except that today she was wearing something tight and lime.

'Come in for a coffee,' she called. 'I've just dropped Tristan and Isadora at day care and I've got half an hour before my aerobics class.'

And you could have knocked me down with a toilet brush when she ushered me into the biggest, shiniest family room I'd ever seen.

SLEEPING Over-Time

Troshus and Rash had been enjoying just another little guys' afternoon, reducing the life expectancy of the azaleas and hunting a few feral lizards, but I was relieved that it was coming to an end.

Troshus is one of those children who remind you of a bank account . . . best in small deposits. Definitely not the sort of child you'd be interested in if you were considering a long-term investment at fixed interest.

Then, just as his mother pulled into the driveway to make the withdrawal, Rash levelled his dreaded big guns at me and staged the worst kind of emotional hold-up.

'Hey Mum,' he cried pleadingly, his blackened eye limpid with longing, 'can Troshus sleep over? Remember, it's OUR turn to have HIM.'

When I was a little girl, back in the dark ages before tracksuits had been invented and when the children who wore joggers to school were the poor ones, sleeping over was an unheard of luxury.

Even having a friend for a meal used to be a big treat. If it ever came off at all, we took photos with the box brownie and made a special trip to the shop for crusty bread and an extra three slices of ham.

Even then it was only ever lunch. No mere playmate was invited for dinner. That was an honour reserved for our pinching, hair-oiled cousins who came twice a year.

By the time I began dabbling my toes in the messy waters of motherhood, all this had changed. Rarely did my children's friends come to our house between the convenient hours which separated breakfast and lunch or lunch and tea. Extra bread and peanut butter had always to be available for the inevitable shared meal. It didn't take long for me to realise that even though no Storm child would come within spitting distance of Vegemite, I needed a biggish jar of the stuff in my cupboard to meet the tastes of the passing parade of luncheon guests.

Our bread, which is beige and has teeny weeny little bits of fibre in it, has never been acceptable. We always strike children who eat only the pure white sliced variety, preferably with the crusts cut off, or we find we are feeding the scornful offspring of health fanatics who are used to that bread where every slice is full of boulders and weighs more than a bible.

Lunch is difficult, but providing dinner is a disaster. Faced with a typical Storm family meal of meat and three veg, visiting children have been known to lose the power to chew. Unless I oblige their companions with plastic pies, chicken nuggets or the right brand of pizza, Turbulence, Serenity and Rash face a bleak future, forever labelled as the kids whose mother serves sensible food at a sleepover.

Apart from feeding overnight guests, there is the problem of actually getting them to retire for sleep. I did not use the term 'getting them to bed' because rarely does sleeping over involve beds. Sleeping bags are essential and many parents believe that's all children need. Yet I find myself unable to say to a visiting child: 'Just pull up a piece of floor and climb on'.

Call me old-fashioned, but I like to offer them the fold-up bed, or a mattress or at least some cushions arranged in a sleep-shaped rectangle.

It's amazing how many children will tell you that their mother doesn't make them brush their teeth at night. Or in the morning either, if it comes to that, unless the mood takes them. The speed of their ablutions astonishes me as well. You hand them one of your best towels and a clean face washer and they're back out of your bathroom before you've had time to close the door of the linen cupboard. My children are incredibly impressed with friends who are able to wash so quickly that not a drop of water actually hits the sink.

A lot of other fluid hits the porcelain however. From the minute the light goes out and all the noisy night long, guests who sleep over have to visit the toilet. Long after the sun goes down, hours after the moon comes out and on and on into the grey and chalky morning, Nature calls them from their bed/floor/cushions into the apparent fascination of our bathroom.

The only silver lining in the sleeping bag, as I watched Troshus's mother back joyfully down my driveway with her investment still intact, was the thought of having a brief break from her son in the near future. Sleeping over is guaranteed to destroy friendships. I presume this is because everyone involved in a sleepover is so foul after approximately two hours' interrupted sleep that they hate the world and each other for weeks afterwards.

This particular night went as they always do. The giggling and squealing stopped eventually, the thumping ceased at last, the pillow fights, the sleeping bag races and the wrestling slowly died away. But inevitably and inexorably, the visits to the toilet went on until dawn.

And they flushed every time!

A MOST ENDANGERED Species

They are still being bred in captivity but every year their numbers are reduced. They don't die; they just shed their thin external skins and slip quietly away.

Many are attracted from their natural habitat into offices and centres of business; others stay close to their nests, having learned from experience the danger of being lured too close to schools.

They are one of Australia's greatest national resources — they are her Helping Mothers. But like many of our natural treasures, they've been exploited and drained dry. They are on the way out.

Small numbers of Helping Mothers can still be found in isolated pockets, slicing and serving in canteens, supervising sport, listening to reading, selling cakes, covering limp library books, training teams, dunking lamingtons in coconut, and counting money for book clubs and banking.

There's one feature these women share which has equipped them to last longer than the weaker ones of the species. They have developed thicker skins . . .

'Oh no!' shrieked Tracy Tong as I sat down beside her on the bus. 'Did you feel how the coach sank down on this side when YOU got in?'

'We all had to wear sun cream on our noses but you didn't because you've got make-up slapped on everywhere, haven't you?' said Ben. 'Anyway, that's what my mother said to Mrs Brisk at the gate.'

'My little brother's got plastic sneakers just like yours,' said James.

Nowhere is the Helping Mother worked so hard and appreciated so little as on school excursions.

Unsung and unpaid, each HM is allocated six or seven small charges and instructed to keep them safe, happy, well-informed and above the law, for hours at a time. This can be accurately translated as taking the children to the toilet as often as possible and making frequent food stops.

Revolutionary acts such as showing them what they are meant to be seeing, or attempting to instruct them in any way, are futile. No matter where you are, sixty per cent will have already been there, (and had a much better time than you're giving them) and forty per cent will be much more interested in the ice block stall, the toilets, the helicopter overhead and you.

The zoo is a popular choice for school excursions. Helping mothers have been heard to wonder why, as the latest trend in zoo decor ensures that while the animals are happy and contented in their absolutely natural habitat, almost none of them can be seen by visitors.

The children love the zoo. Relieved of the necessity of actually looking at anything, they can concentrate on themselves.

'I have a pain but food usually makes it go away,' said Tracy. 'Where's the toilet?'

'There are possums in here,' I said, studiously reading the notes obligingly provided by the teacher. 'They sleep during the day and wake up at night. They are back to front animals.'

'You mean they're nocturnal,' said Ben.

'I'm hungry,' said Tracy. 'I need the toilet.'

'These lizards are almost extinct,' I quoted.

'That means they smell awful,' said Allison. 'Like a toilet.'

'Koala bears are native to Australia,' I read.

'They haven't wiped their bottoms,' said James. 'Weren't we looking for a toilet?'

'Look at the camel's eyelashes,' I said. 'They're very thick, to protect the camel's eyes in sand storms in the desert.'

'Look at it doing wee,' said Sam. 'Is there a toilet near here?'

A mutual instinct for survival bonds Helping Mothers at the zoo, as they hunt for signs of animal habitation and plumbing. HMs who haven't previously met use their previous networking skills to pool their information.

'Don't muck about with the lion,' advised a woman with a swag of seven small thugs in blue and maroon. 'It hasn't even got a mane and it's asleep. Try the jaguar. It's under a rock over there and you can actually see two legs and part of the tail.'

'The bear is coming out!' shouted a floppy American lady. A tide of spectators rushed to see it (a whole animal! maybe even a whole gay animal!) but the bear changed his mind and loped away from the cooing crowd, disappearing back into the rocks. He knew which side HIS honeycomb was buttered on.

'Can we move on now?' asked Tracy. 'I have to go again.'

The other recurrent theme for five-year-olds at the zoo is death.

'Look at the elephants, children. They have trunks and tusks. What do you think they use the tusks for?'

'To kill people. Can we go to the toilet?'

'Look at the beautiful peacock just there on the grass.'

'If he bit me would I die?' asked Rash.

The fairy penguins were dainty fuzz balls turning sleek in the aqua water.

'If I went swimming with them would they peck me to death?' asked Ben. 'If you've finished looking at them,' said Tracy, 'I need to go to the toilet again.'

When we had all eaten our squashed sandwiches we found we had extra time. 'I suppose we have to look at some more rocks in cages,' said Rash despondently. 'We might find the giraffe,' I said. 'It's hard for a giraffe to hide.' 'Couldn't we go back to that drink machine instead?' asked Sam.

On the way home the air in the bus was thick with warmth and the fragrance of hot banana skins. My legs ached, my head buzzed, and I allowed my tired eyes to close.

I awoke to find several of my party hanging over the back of the seat in front of me, staring at my face with breathless fascination.

'Her bottom lip hangs down like an elephant's,' said James.

'Her hair is all spiky on top like a monkey's,' said Ben.

'Her eyelids are all wrinkled like that big old camel,' said my son.

'She couldn't kill you,' said Tracy cheerfully, 'because she hasn't got tusks.'

They'd learned a lot more than I thought. Except that like the rest of my species, I was about to become extinct.

THE ONE DAY War

A ceasefire is operating. Peace talks are under way as the last of the rations is shared between those on the home front. The enemy has left. Our house has been liberated.

Rash's birthday is over for another year.

The roar of the battle still rings in my ears, my temples ache from sleepless nights preparing for the attack and I can still taste the sticky sweetness of excess icing as it clings to my gritted teeth.

The main problem with holding birthday parties is that children have to come to them. Usually, that means war.

The preliminary skirmish usually happens a week or so before the big day, when you try to sort out the guest list. Take the advice Bob Dylan sang in that song protesting against the futility of war: don't criticise what you can't understand. Listen to your child. Remember, he or she has seen these kids in action, in the classroom, in their homes, on the roads and in the trenches.

Serenity once made a guest list which included every girl in her class except one. Horrified at her heartlessness I insisted that the girl she called Ghastly Greta be asked to come. My usually kind and sensitive little person glared at me. 'You'll be sorry,' she said.

Within five minutes of arriving, Ghastly Greta had told me that she was much more beautiful than my child because her mother had said so. Within ten minutes she had given the dog a Chinese burn and bitten the baby. She had a terrific asthma attack on the lawn when she only found three lollies in the Mintie hunt; massive tears trickled down her cheeks whenever she didn't win a game and just before throwing up on the cream rug she stood on the face of the birthday doll.

I have never criticised my children's guest lists since.

Like the day before any battle, the one before the birthday party involves campaign planning (aim for survival of the parents) and the preparation of camouflage (something they can wear which might persuade them they are participating in a celebration rather than an attack) and rations.

A party with theme clothes and decorations is memorable and impresses the sensible mothers who take the easy way out and invite everyone to join them at Mackers, but again you have to consider the size of the invasion. Making one fairy crown is fun; stapling 22 cardboard stars to 22 strips of foil and discovering that your fingers are permanently moulded together at the tips with gluey glitter, is not.

Like the banner you carry into battle, the cake has to be reasonably inspiring. A round cake with a plastic footballer or ballet dancer on the top is a safe bet, but I am one of those soldiers so desperate to be decorated that I spend party mornings up to my elbows in icing, trying to make cakes which look like rocket missiles or Olympic gymnasts.

With enough smarties you can simulate almost anything; but first you've got to get the icing to stay on the cake. It's a carefully coded secret that forcing a woman to ice the sides of a cake, any cake, is an internationally recognised form of torture. Only sleep deprivation is a more effective tool in the destruction of self-confidence.

There is always the danger of cakes which have shortened your life expectancy going unrecognised on the big day. On one occasion I laboured over a sleek white and silver jet plane cake, in keeping with the aeroplane theme which had also kept me up for weeks making ten little blue and silver pilots' hats from crepe paper and a year's supply of sticky tape. A tall boy burst through my door wearing his own personalised flying helmet, goggles and leather pilot's gloves. He made straight for the cake and turned up his nose.

'I thought this was an aircraft party,' he said scornfully. 'What's with the fat fish?'

One parent at least will go for the surprise tactic — her child will always arrive early. When you hear the cry: 'Someone's here!' the invasion begins.

The birthday battle is fought inside as well as outside. It shakes your windows and rattles your walls and even before the gifts are all unwrapped, it's raging.

The crackle and crunch of presents and paper fills your ears as you lunge desperately between small bodies, trying to keep the cards (why?), striving to save the face and feelings of the unfortunates whose mothers made them bring books, screaming that now is NOT the moment to try the new face-paint (whoever this parent is SHE MUST HATE YOU) and begging the boys and girls to postpone putting the 100-piece constucta-gun together until after pass the parcel.

There's always someone who screams, someone who sulks, someone who cheats, someone who doesn't want to play any of the games, someone who wants to go home and someone who keeps winning everything. There's always one child who sicks/poohs/wheezes early in the party and has to be attended to, which is when the others go and eat the prizes. There is always someone who is allergic to food colouring or artificial flavouring.

A great deal has been written about what children eat at parties but there's not much mention of what they leave behind, mashed into the wreckage of your colour coordinated serviettes.

They don't eat the cake. Or if they do they don't eat the icing. They put round cheese things on their fingers, crush them under the chairs and roll them around the table but they rarely put them in their mouths. They don't eat the bottom half of meringues, the edges of pizzas, the lids of pies, the crusts of sandwiches or the second tray of sausage rolls. They don't eat the quaint little cheese and sultana men you made to introduce a note of nutrition.

They're at war. They need energy fast. They eat the lollies.

When the cavalry comes to collect the victors, your own child is almost certainly crying, if not heavily involved in a really juicy tantrum. He wants nothing to do with handing out lumps of soggy cakes, he's not interested in uncurling writhing balloon strings so each guest can take one home (why?), or presenting party souvenirs.

This year, in my perverse post-party maternal mood, I understand and sympathise. The war was fought in his name and he has taken a fair amount of booty, but now that it is over he is battle-weary and fatigued; he hasn't made any genuine territorial gains — as old as he has become, he is still the youngest and smallest person in the house.

He walks slowly to his room, dragging his feet through a sticky plate of half-eaten lamingtons which is lying in the hall. But I bark no orders. I let him retreat without a court martial.

Sometimes war is like that.

Growling

I've been a tiger for three hours this morning and I'm depressed.

I know I shouldn't be. I know I am three times blessed with healthy children (if you don't count colds, impetigo, hay fever, asthma, allergies, constipation and about $9,000 worth of potential orthodontic problems) and I have a comfortable, curly husband whose only vice is to fall asleep when I am speaking to him. I have a writing job which pays for school shoes and petrol and if I'm careful, doughnuts on Fridays; I have my own car (which is leaking oil over the new pavers); in seventeen years we'll own our own home; I'm not pregnant and I'm not in the Mother's Club.

So why am I depressed?

What right have I, leading my fortunate and comfortable suburban middle class life, to give in to misery, to argue with my mother when she holds up my silver lining and suggests that if I've got nothing better to do than moan, I'd be better off washing and ironing it before I put it away for the winter.

Do I want to go out and get a proper job? No. How could I bare to miss witnessing the daily discoveries of my lovable Rash as he grows from babyhood into an individual, independent little person, who gags dolls, ties their hands and feet with pipe cleaners and stuffs them down the toilet?

I want to be here for the big ones when they get home after a hard day's learning; I want to be the one who hears how many people hate them this week and what video they watched while the teacher did some marking. I want to be the one whose heart swells with tender affection when they burst through the door crying heartily: 'Hi! What's to eat and it better not be apples!'

And yet even when I don't read the papers, I'm still depressed.

My doctor says it's hormones. She has this plan to put the entire female population of Australia on the pill for life in order to alleviate premenstrual and pre-menopausal problems. But the prospect of still getting my period when I'm ninety makes me depressed.

I'm depressed because Rash won't do anything he's told unless I am Mother Tiger; the growling hurts my throat and makes me feel as if I haven't given up smoking. Again.

I'm depressed because my children's orthodontist told me that nowadays, when people have a smile like mine, they can have an operation.

I'm depressed because the neighbour's cat has visited my sandpit again and the money I'm saving by not having a pet is going on worm medicine because my neighbour does.

I'm depressed because Serenity has converted six old wine bottles into ballerinas, with pink curly paper, felt pen, glue and curling ribbon, and now she wants to keep them on the mantelpiece, beside the Good Husband's trophy for Irish darts. She's lost all the lids of the felt pens again and they're bleeding rainbows on her feather quilt which isn't washable.

I'm depressed because when I tell people my husband won a trophy in an Irish darts competition, they always think I'm joking.

I'm depressed because my friend, Moana, has put her two-year-old, Little Grabbi-Anne, into Daycare, where she is being constantly stimulated, while Rash sits here, ignoring his educational toys and watching soap operas while I type and growl.

My husband is trying to think of something we could have all given up for Lent.

I'm depressed because I can't show ten-year-old Turbulence how to do his sums.

I'm depressed because he got into the district swimming finals which means I have to spend another day at the council pool, watching him swim for 49.1 seconds and queue for canteen sweets for six hours.

I'm depressed because my mother says I use Santa Claus like other people use machine guns.

I'm depressed because three weeks ago my best potted fern was lush and green like the ones in 'Days of our Lives' and now every day of my life it sheds another clump of leaves onto the carpet.

I'm depressed because Serenity is heartbroken that her favourite friend blocks her ears whenever she goes past. Her other friend makes sick-up noises when she sits near her on the bus. I am to blame for all of it, since I advised her to ignore them last Monday, when all they had done was stick out their tongues.

I'm depressed because the man who serviced my sewing machine (when all I wanted was a quote so that I could decide that sewing my children's clothes would not be economical) told me it's people like me who make him wish he'd been a brain surgeon.

I'm depressed because all my friends have part-time jobs which they hadn't planned to take, but just couldn't say no to because the conditions were exactly what a mother with three children dreams of, whereas my part-time job is the only one I can do.

I'm depressed because the house needs painting, there are enormous grey bald spots in the lawn, I haven't written the Great Australian Novel yet, something sticky has been spilled in the back of the pantry, black things are eating my azaleas and I heard the children plotting to cook me a birthday cake all by themselves.

I'm depressed because my husband, my mother and my closest friends are trivialising my depression. They think the only reason I'm miserable is because I turn forty next week.

Surely they don't believe a little thing like that could worry a great big old tiger like me?

LETTER FROM QUITE A BIG *Helper*

1 Frustration Close
Treestump South
December 10

Dear Santa Claus,

I do hope this reaches you before the rush, because what I have to say is too important to relegate to the secretarial elves, particularly as I suspect they have gone over to computers.

Heaven forbid that I should tear Your Jolliness away from all that last minute carving, not to mention stripe-painting of giant candy canes, especially when it's so difficult to do with frostbitten fingers, but please spare a thought for all your middle-sized helpers down here in the Antipodes, who are doing their best to enhance your reputation in temperatures which would melt reindeer bells. Believe me, sweaty fingers are incompatible with sewing sequins on the dancing dress for the Christmas concert and at least YOU do not have to worry about your make-up sliding off your face and staining the Superman cape on the sewing machine.

Santa, I am a devoted fan. I was still scanning the sky for a sign of your sleigh long after my thirty-fifth birthday. But in your efforts to keep up with the times, I'm afraid you are giving yourself a serious credibility problem.

When I was a child it was normal for kids to develop a certain cynicism about your actual existence about the time they graduated from shorts to long trousers. I don't know if you realise it, Your Fuzziness, but these days children are lucky if they still believe in you when they climb out of their last nappy!

To rectify the problem, I'd like to draw Your Twinkling's attention to the main areas of discontent. First, those candy canes. Oh, the children don't mind sucking pure, artificially flavoured sugar for hours on end on the 25th of December, but can't you see that it tempts them to play you off against their dentist? Santa, you should be setting a good example. I've already told them your weight problem is hormonal. And by the way, is it sensible to ride a sleigh at breakneck speed around the world in one night without wearing a seat belt?

Apart from that, not a single child of my acquaintance has ever finished a candy cane. They sit on saucers in the fridge until Easter, growing slowly soggier until not even the cockroaches are interested in them.

The main problem, however, is the extra presents you leave for my children on Christmas Day.

Truly, the Big Present is never a problem. The children put their orders in early for whatever their annual ambition turns out to be and then they sit back in their imported sneakers and relax, secure in the knowledge that providing they don't answer back, introduce four letter words into the household or forget to tidy their rooms on Christmas Eve, the desired gift will magically appear before them in the lounge room on the following morning.

The good thing about Big Presents is that the children generally provide so many details about brand names, colours and styles that you, Santa, (do you mind if I call you by your first name?) almost always come up with exactly the right goods.

But for many lucky children, one present is not enough. Seething around the boogy board or bike there are always a lot of other competing parcels, brightly and laboriously wrapped, and containing, I'm afraid to tell you, a whole lot of presents which are doomed to a boring life in the toy cupboard or wardrobe, until such time as they can be decently donated to charity by children pretending they have been struck by the following year's Christmas spirit.

Which brings me back to the subject of the carving and painting. You may as well stop now, Santa, because never in my history as a parent have I seen any child playing with a brightly painted wooden toy. What? They are supposed to pull it along? Santa, Santa, that only happens in the pages of storybooks, where even the boy children wear buckle-up shoes. And speaking of books, I wouldn't bother printing any more unless you can provide them with peep flaps on every second page, and bits of cardboard that they can tear out or pull off.

Listen, Your Heartiness, all those pretty dolls are wildly out of date. Ugly dolls with malformed limbs, who boast neither eyelashes nor sweetly pouting lips are the only kind which go over well with little girls these days. It's probably something to do with self-esteem. My generation all grew up feeling ugly because of the perfection of our doll's faces, but our daughters have it all worked out — compared to her Cabbage Patch even the most toothless terror looks appealing.

The weapons are a waste. They usually snap in half before New Year and only the ones which make loud, guttural noises last for eternity. A big stick from the yard is always better. But apart from that, doesn't giving guns, swords and axes make a bit of a mockery of this peace on earth stuff? How do you teach a child to play economic sanctions when he has a machine gun in his hands?

Anything that works with batteries has been banned from this house for years and yet you always bring more of them. Even in the unlikely event that the original batteries will actually be replaced, these will not stay inside the toy, because by then the sliding flap which holds them in place will have long disappeared into the bowels of the toy box, together with the Chinese checkers and refugee draftsmen.

Speaking of games, Santa, could we have a year off? No doubt there's nothing you and the elves enjoy more on Boxing Day than a cosy game of Trivial Pursuit, but there are more people available at your place. Boxed board games of every kind require two or more players and if war games are to be avoided, at least one player has to be over eighteen.

How many times have you had to collect six tonnes of wrapping paper, make four beds, change three nappies, toss a salad, hot wand your hair and cook a turkey by midday, while simultaneously keeping control of a dice and a pink plastic counter?

Why do you keep leaving those cellophane bags full of tiny soldiers or plastic animals? Do you honestly think the children are going to breathe the life of imagination into these tiny creatures, when it's all provided for them in magical animation on the television screen?

The problem of clothes as presents just won't go away, Santa. The children have asked me to suggest that you put all the new clothing items in the same parcel, so that they will recognise this as the boring but useful present which can be left until last. Mrs Santa Claus has lately taken to wrapping every garment separately; she has even been known to remove individual socks from their cardboard hook and make them look like two presents.

Then Your Snowiness, there is the problem of price tags. MUST you supplement supplies from your workshop with all those packaged toys from the chain stores? If it's unavoidable, could you please get some elves to remove the price tags BEFORE Christmas Eve? There's nothing unhappier on Christmas morning than a parent who got to bed at two, was woken at five and has to explain the shredded price tags beneath her fingernails at six.

I really think kids these days are getting sick of anti-sexism, Your Rosiness. What's the use of giving all those pink plastic vacuum cleaners to little boys, when they only use them as machine guns anyway? Go back to the trucks and tea sets. At least they are not violent and girls and boys alike are going to have to learn to drive and wash dishes.

Finally, there's the question of felt pens and face washers. No child in the history of the world has ever been excited at receiving a face washer. As for felt pens, we all know times are hard, Your Jollity, but when they say they want a packet of pens, a packet is what they mean. Individually wrapping twelve textas so that it looks as if you're giving them more presents is a cheap trick which encourages an unattractive streak of cynicism even in a four-year-old.

All these appearances by your helpers in malls and shopping centres may be good for the country's unemployment situation, but they are another handicap to your image. Frankly, if you can't come yourself, just send an apology and a mail order catalogue from the North Pole. Relocate the boys in red, especially the thin ones who don't shave yet and the cranky ones who hate kids. Give them a reindeer to renovate or something but if you want to stay real, beware of reality.

As Mrs Claus could probably tell you, Santa, fantasy is much more fun.

Merry Christmas from Your Devoted Helper,

Frances Virginia Storm

Part 2

JUST Kidding

From the age of five, children go out into the big wide world and discover irrefutable evidence that their parents are inferior in almost every department to those of other children. They must either persuade you to change your style to that of Everyone Else's Parents, or resign themselves to an existence as a misjudged minority group of luckless losers whose parents are too poor, too cruel or too stupid to put chocolate bars in their lunch boxes.

You may cling for a little longer to the fantasy that they are just kids and that you know better than they do – but reality is just a scornful shrug away.

GOTTA HAVE Friends

She burst out of the bushes near my parents' brand new house and the impact of her huge white smile almost threw me backwards. I was ten years old and she was the most gorgeous thing that had happened to me in my life. She had glossy black curls, bare feet and plump olive brown limbs crammed into tight pink shorts and she was the unquestioned queen of the local kids.

She was Theresa Populossos, the ripe and cheeky daughter of the couple who owned our local fish and chip shop and the only girl in class to celebrate going into double figures by getting a bra.

I was the new girl, all the way from the city — and in that small country town, temporarily a novelty. I was granted the dazzling honour of becoming her best friend.

Theresa was smarter than me; she rode, ran, danced, sang and stood on her head better than I did. In the class elections, she became Captain and I was merely Vice. I was content to be her loyal shadow until the tragic day when Theresa was in bed with German Measles and I was chosen in her place to lay the Anzac Day wreath at the town war memorial. My brief moment of glory was cancelled out by the pain of being tossed out of Theresa's affections in favour of a juvenile jacks player.

One of the hardest lessons of childhood is that keeping up with your friends doesn't necessarily mean keeping them. Which is why I knew how Serenity felt when she arrived home from school mute with misery.

She dropped her school bag in the middle of the floor where it slumped into a sickening heap and began regurgitating books, stencil sheets and a lunch box smelling of banana skin. Only because her eyes were hot and heartbroken did I resist the urge to go straight into a lecture on the glories of Globite.

Because this was my daughter and not my sons, it took a while but eventually the story seeped out.

'Sky and Fern are the only ones I know in my class except Peace and she says she's going to make a fight with me because I was voted Pupil of the Week.'

She pushed her tears back into her eyes with texta-covered fingers. 'Peace and Hope are making sick-up noises when I walk past. I wish it was still last year.'

We spend so much time making the right choices for our girls and boys — the degree of fibre in their bread, the percentage of cotton in their clothes, plain or striped toothpaste, playdough rather than plasticine, posh or state schools, 'Here's Humphrey' or 'Playschool'. But from the time they can talk, they choose their own friends and there's little most parents can do about it. When the children they adore toss them aside like crumpled tissues, they don't even want you to smooth out the creases.

Serenity is quiet, well-behaved and quite clever; consequently she is destined never to be truly popular at school. When she is not in disgrace for doing well at her work she is taunted for not taking sides during the continuing round of fights which little girls use to break up the monotony of their school days. Is it any wonder that she prefers to spend her time with the people she builds out of the cardboard tubes from toilet rolls and plastic wrap? I comfort myself with the thought that by making her own recyclable friends she is helping to save the environment. And at least I don't have to drive them home and have coffee with their mothers.

The first term of school is the worst time for friendships. A quaint form of torture still employed by most primary schools is the mixing up of old classes at the beginning of each year so that established friendships are carelessly crushed; theoretically, fresh classes are supposed to create fresh friends, but the result is the same stale situation that occurs at this time every year.

Because she is a Good and Sensible Girl it takes Serenity the better part of a year to break in another Good and Sensible Girl who shares her passion for craft, works conscientiously at school and doesn't drown her in conversation. These friendships are tenuous because it's often these Good and Sensible Girls who are the high achievers who don't appreciate too much competition. Secretly, Serenity longs for a friendship with a Silly Girl, but this is unlikely to happen until she learns to giggle. And occasionally, to utter whole sentences at a time.

Turbulence has never been bothered by competition but nor did he have a best friend at primary school. Instead he had a hero.

Blade had a satin fringe, enormous vacant eyes and was congenitally incapable of comprehending any form of adult speech unless it contained single syllable words and was repeated at least twice.

He lived opposite our house for ten years before his family moved away and Turbulence adored the ground he loped on.

In vain did I spend hours of my life telephoning women with sons of suitable age and behaviour, inviting them to come and play with Turb. In vain did I bribe them with ice blocks and football cards, with building cubbies and having extra goes. All I got for my pains was the sort of recognition that results from knowing so many women at the school that you are the first person they think of when they want helpers for the lamington drive.

Blade was three years older than Turbulence, and when he cycled off to school each day on his BMX, Turb would wheel his bicycle with its shiny training wheels down to the gate and sit on it while he patiently waited for the arrival home of his hero.

When Blade came back, he would flick his fringe in Turb's direction and disappear inside his own house. He would emerge five minutes later with a fistful of artificially flavoured food, leap on his battered bike and ride off again, with Turb's eyes burrowing into his laconic backbone.

Blade made his own snacks and was allowed to ride on the road. Blade never had to change out of his school uniform at the end of the day. Blade had never in his life worn leather school shoes or been required home at a particular time; he was rarely seen holding the handle bars of his bike with anything other than one hand.

In the time we lived opposite to Blade, he broke both his arms, one of his legs, burnt his arm, cracked two ribs and was rushed to hospital once for taking a bite out of a pine tree. The only thing he had in common with Turbulence was accidents. Turb was always worrying that one might happen. Blade was always on his way to one.

It was a great relief that Serenity never developed a strong affection for Nikky Next Door, who is the same age as she is, but seems to be much older. When she was little she preferred games which involved removing clothes. You could understand it when they played hospitals, but why did she have to take off her knickers to do a jigsaw puzzle?

Nikky has always reminded me a little of Theresa Populossos. She could swim before anyone else, she could work herself up on a swing, run, ride, handstand, cartwheel and climb better than any other kid. Whenever I see Nikky lately, she is hanging upside down from something. From which it is obvious that she now keeps her pants on.

Nikky is a most adaptable child and will play with any or all of our children. Everyone likes her. Shop assistants know her by name, bus drivers pull up and uncomplainingly allow their mumbling motors to idle while she wanders across the road in front of them, wearing her skimpy shift, flicking her skimpy hair. She is polite but offhand. She is invited everywhere. What does this child have, I can't help but ask myself, that other girls don't?

Whatever it is, I want Serenity to have it too.

Like every street, we also have Gordon. The Gordons of this world were not made to live in their own homes, nor do they have any toys of their own with which they care to play. They have little charm and are not generally blessed with beauty; we are looking forward to the day our Gordon is old enough to visit his orthodontist. But Gordons are tidy and reliable. You can certainly rely on them to keep coming over.

Our children learned early that Gordon came in handy for taking ice block sticks to the bin, putting away the blocks, disconnecting the track and sorting out the puzzle pieces after the toddler had muddled them up. No matter what my children have ever done to Gordon, even if they have sent him home for unforgivable dullness, left him stranded in the Jacaranda or ridden over his nylon cat, he has always come back. Each of our children grew into him and then grew out of him again but still he is available. In the years to come, Gordon will be the first kid in the street to get a car and no doubt we will all continue to find him useful.

With his huge circle of school friends, our youngest child Rash COULD be a truly popular child. But Rash is a winner. If anyone wants to be his best friend, they will have to make sure they are second best at everything else.

I should know. That's how I won Theresa back!

A LITTLE Reality

A parent's life is full of unanswerable questions.

There's: If I tell him about the Easter Bunny, will he think I'm a liar when he discovers the truth? And: Is he really sick or does he just want to miss the mathematics test? Or: If I smack her in the middle of the supermarket will all these other parents think I'm a bad mother? As opposed to: If I let her keep screaming and biting the shopping trolley will all these parents think I'm a bad mother?

But the one question which I have asked myself most in the last year or ten is: 'Why don't my children use their imagination?'

We have done everything in our limited parent power to encourage Turbulence, Serenity and Rash to discover the wonders of fantasy. We have read to them until our tired eyes could barely focus on the texta-scribbled page, we have risked life and limb hanging mobiles from their ceilings, decorating their rooms with inspirational pictures, pointing out the secrets of sea shells and rocks and cliffs and beaches and wondering aloud about the secret imaginary antics of Santa and the elves, forest gnomes, bush babies, extinct dragons, That Rabbit and our family favourite, the rice bubble fairy.

It's no use. Huge supplies of imagination are gathering mould in their minds, while in the meantime they apply themselves to the serious reality of living.

How would they have survived all their weekends and holidays, I asked myself, without man-made entertainments like the swimming pool, the television set and the computer? Why did they never play games where they pretended to be grown up, to be brave, to be bold, to be beautiful?

'You told me I'm already beautiful,' said Serenity.

'You said I was brave and bold,' said Rash.

'Grown ups have too much to worry about,' said Turbulence.

On one long and lazy afternoon I came into the house after my daily liaison with the clothesline to find Rash hunched over the computer. His face was flinty and his mouth was set in a grim, determined line as he attempted to annihilate the tiny non-humans on the screen; his button finger may have been fit and muscular, I told him, but his body would soon be slack and soft.

In the next room his sister Serenity stared with glazed eyes at the television and up the hall their big brother Turbulence was arranging his cassettes into a complex filing system with cross references relating to the year each was purchased, the rating he gave each group and the level of obscenity obvious in each song. (The latter category enables him to choose which ones are suitable for playing in the car.)

I began to rant and rave, in the way all the books I use for reference for my More Serious Articles tell parents never to do. Why couldn't they get out in the fresh air, I asked. Why couldn't they play in our large, busy garden which was full of potential cubbies, fabulous hiding places and faraway trees which almost speared the clouds and sent roots underground to turn our driveway into rubble? What was the point of having rubble-causing roots if children were not playing imaginative games in the trees above?

Rash looked up from his game of death and told me in the prolonged whining tone of the standard eight-year-old that the yard was also full of potentially painful bindi-eyes and the trees were full of bees. 'I don't want to hunt bees,' he said plaintively. 'They sting back.'

Turbulence raised his eyes to their parent-addressing position in the top of his head. 'I've been in the fresh air,' he said. 'I've had a swim. It's not good to be out in the ultraviolet rays for too long. And I'm too old for make-believe.'

The trouble with Turb is that he's always been too old for make-believe.

Instead he files. At four he filed his stacking cups, at five his puzzles, at eight it was his Lego. Now he files cassettes. Filing is safe, organised and free from the threat of ultraviolet and ultra-violence.

'Serenity,' I cried, ripping the cord of the television out of the wall. 'Go and do something with your imagination. Play mothers and fathers or doctors and nurses or bosses and secretaries or something.'

Serenity sighed as only Serenity can, and raised herself slowly from her comfortable couch. 'They're all such sexist concepts, Mum,' she muttered, but went upstairs to my office and shut the door.

Half an hour later, having worked myself up into the sort of anxiety attack which was doubtless going to shorten my life expectancy, I put up my radar and went on a spot check for obvious signs of imagination.

Serenity was upstairs using the computer. But as I opened my pursed lips to scream, she whirled around in the swivel chair they had all given me for Mother's Day. (I had asked for something that would make me smell nice. They explained that the chair would eliminate perspiration odour by cutting down on my movements; besides it was more fun for them.)

'I'm playing secretaries,' she said. 'I'm pretending to do what the girls do at Dad's office. Except I'm being a boy secretary and my boss is a woman.'

Turbulence was standing in front of his mirror holding a tennis racquet in his arms like a newborn child. A tape was playing loudly in his machine. 'I'm using my imagination,' he said. 'I'm pretending I'm a famous rock singer and girls are screaming at me and throwing their clothes onto the stage.'

'I thought the stars threw THEIR clothes at the girls,' I said.

'I don't have to go overboard on this, do I Mum?' he replied. 'You wouldn't want me to catch cold.'

In the family room, Rash had replaced Serenity in front of the television set. His eyes were glazed, his bottom lip hung slack, as if the hinge on his mouth had broken.

The television cord still lay unconnected on the floor and the screen was blank, but I had to roar his name twice before he pulled his gaze away from the magic box.

'Sorry Mum,' he said. 'I was pretending to watch television. You were right. All it takes is a little imagination.'

INTERNAL Affairs

There are two big secrets The Sisterhood keep from you when you decide to have a family.

First, of course, there's childbirth. You never find out until it's too late how long it takes and how much it hurts.

The second secret is that never in the history of western civilisation have children been known to voluntarily clean their rooms.

Nevertheless, when springtime comes, a young mum's fancy turns to washing curtains and cleaning out cupboards — and older mums, being even more fanciful, decide it's time their children helped.

While curtain washing will doubtless ever be my responsibility, I decided this particular spring that the equally awful chore of cleaning out cupboards could be delegated. Surely if our children want to be unique and independent they should have the unique responsibility of independently keeping their own possessions in order?

In the course of my research into one of my More Serious Stories I read that a respected academic said mothers should be less concerned about their children's untidy habits. It was more important to raise children to be kind and considerate towards others, than to put pressure on them to keep their rooms neat.

I would like this man to live in Serenity's room for one week. (Maybe he could squeeze in beside the hairy bears, tigers and rabbits, the solar system chart, the purple basset hound, the witch's hat and the school project on wool that's been on top of her cupboard for three years.) I would like to persuade him that the most welcome act of kindness and consideration a child can perform is to present a tidy room to a mother.

Never in her life has Serenity been known to close a cupboard door. Never has she bent her body from the waist to pick up a garment. The phrases 'fold up', 'sort out' and 'get a hanger' are as foreign to her as Latin verbs. Asked to tidy her room, Serenity will stand in the doorway, faced with overflowing drawers, an orgy of clothing on the carpet, boxes and shoes falling out of every storage space, and a desk on which a dozen books vie for space with assorted sized paper, texta pens and three years of Brownie craft work. She will study the scene for a moment with a perplexed frown, and then, with a sudden smile of relief, pounce on a hair elastic which has been wound around the bedpost, transfer it to a heap of scrunchies which are choking on hair on top of her dressing table, and leave the room with the satisfaction of seeing a job well done.

The spring school holidays seemed as suitable a time as any for the Storm children to learn the art of sorting new from old, of recognising the difference between what was mess and what was precious (last year's pine cone collection versus plaster of Paris models of five-year-old hands), of getting rid of such things as wine bottles dressed as ballerinas to make room in their cupboards for the future delights that birthdays and Christmases (aaaaargh!) might bring.

None of our children were impressed with my spring resolution, although their reasons for objecting varied, as did the way they eventually attacked their task.

Turbulence didn't want to clean out his cupboard because as he quite rightly pointed out, it was already as neat as the proverbial pin, if you can imagine a pin with each of its pieces labelled and filed.

Everything Turbulence has ever treasured or collected is still intact and has its own special position in his cupboard and drawers. Move a model car a centimetre to the right and prepare to die. Alter the angle of a Lego construction or touch the adjacent carefully labelled box of emergency bits and expect no mercy.

In the end he took everything out, wiped down all the shelves and drawers and put everything back in exactly the same places.

Rash's objection to spring cleaning was that he suddenly wanted to do as I was always suggesting, and play outside. Forced to reconsider this statement by the pleasant expression on his mother's loving face, he retired grumpily to his room and began work.

Two hours later, thrilled by the sounds of hard labour, I looked in to find Rash sitting on his floor in the middle of a mountain of broken and forgotten toys. A handle-less skipping rope hung around his neck and he wore last year's Easter ice cream container on his head. Tractors, cars, blocks, money boxes, train tracks, racing circuits, guns without barrels, swords without handles, robots without heads, boats, buckets and books were heaped on every available square centimetre of floor space.

'I'd forgotten all this,' Rash announced joyfully. 'Now I can start playing with it all over again, like it was new!'

He brandished something large and ugly which took two hands to hold. 'I even found this mediaeval castle — remember how Serenity helped me make it out of egg cartons, so the lizards can live in it?'

But the boys' efforts were a mere drop in a cracked plastic bucket when compared with the job ahead of their sister.

Cleaning out Serenity's cupboards was an adventure of discovery and complexity in uncharted waters, not unlike Captain Cook's voyage in search of the Great South Land. I gave in and helped her. When we finished, we had a whole new continent to explore and populate and of course, she began at once.

'Now I've got some room I'm going to dress those empty cordial bottles like the people out of *Strictly Ballroom* and stand them on my windowsill.'

I went out into the spring sunset and found the egg carton castle on the veranda, complete with a new extension made from toilet roll cylinders. Rash was catching lizards and moving them into their summer residence.

I thought of letting them in on the Sisterhood's secrets before they had their babies. But I didn't. Why should lizards be warned when mothers are not?

THE CANTEEN Crisis

She wore a green scrunchy on the end of her braid and her skinny fingers were folded, claw-like, around a cluster of coins.

'Please can I have a licketty-split, two Have-a-Bites, a buttered bun with Vegemite and three doughnuts. And a pencil rubber.'

The roar of crowding children filled my ears and my mind went blank. It always does.

You hear the bell. Then the children begin to trickle from the distant buildings, growing like locusts in numbers and noise, until they merge into a throbbing, yelling mass of uniforms.

'Don't serve until you see the whites of their eyes,' mutters my supervisor.

Working in the school canteen has the same effect on me as heavy artillery fire has on soldiers in trenches. It numbs my brain, it cramps my stomach and it turns my legs to liquorice.

'That was two licketty-splits . . .' I began nervously, but the disdainful scowl on the small face across the counter was enough to tell me I was already wrong.

After three years of canteen duty I can sometimes cope with two purchases at a time, providing the cost ends in even numbers. I know enough tables to sometimes manage as many as three, providing it's three of the same thing . . .

But throw orders of four or more at me and the battle is lost. As if adding up the cost and locating everything they want isn't enough, there's the horrible prospect of having to work out the change. And what about that cunning trick where you count backwards . . . or is it forwards? . . . while placing the correct tender into the outstretched palm? It goes with riding a two-wheeler bike as something I've never mastered.

I'm even more pathetic when faced with a small blond angel who opens his grimy hand to reveal a minute silver piece and says: 'What can I buy for this many?'

I cannot bear the anguish of telling him all he can afford is a bread stick.

I have enormous admiration for the women who can add up under pressure and never feel sorry for the children who don't bring enough money. Like doctors' receptionists and the officials who sell tokens at fun fairs, these flinty-eyed, iron-hearted women are able to reject even the most pathetic cases, ordering them to the end of the queue if they're not quick thinkers, or simply sending them emptily away.

It is mothers like my supervisor, Jan Tank, who can do long division in their heads, who demand good manners and rapid orders from even the smallest of their customers, and who know how many pizzas to thaw and where meat pies come from and when the nugget supplies need topping up and whether the baker's wife has had her baby yet.

I never know these things.

In a total reversal of my normal behaviour, when I am working at the canteen, I keep very quiet and do what I am told.

My children are amazed. They queue up on canteen days, just to gaze at my closed, trembling lips, and they lean on the counter with their chins in their hands, smiling wonderingly into my glazed eyes until Jan Tank sends them briskly away.

Daringly they return with twenty-six classmates each, all of whom have forgotten their ice block money. There but for Mrs Tank would go all my housekeeping allowance for the week.

I keep quiet because, for one thing, I have to concentrate. As I line the ancient ovens with low-price foil, I have to memorise the new prices. I have to plug into the concept that a plain crackerbread may only be ten cents but a crackerbread with peanut butter has now gone up to thirteen.

For another thing, I am very frightened of Jan Tank. Between slashing salad for the sandwiches and bagging piles of pies, she has assassinated more characters than you'd find in the New Testament. She is a woman with whom it's wise only to agree.

The headmaster once argued with Mrs Tank; in the interests of nutrition, he wanted us to stop selling iced doughnuts. He had to resign the following term. Mrs Tank, with tomato sauce on her hands, made no secret of her triumph.

This month I arrived at the canteen to find I'd been rostered on with a quivering new young mother, even more inexperienced than me. I saw her lips moving as she tried desperately to memorise the price list before the recess bell rang. I sympathised as poor little Susan braced herself at the counter, watching the hordes come over the hill.

'Two peach-plum-passio poppas, three lick-tubes, a cheese cracker with peanut butter and a whole bun with one side plain and one side buttered. And four liquorice.'

Susan blinked. 'That'll be two dollars and seventy-three cents,' she said, 'and next time you'd better say "please".'

If ever Jan Tank was promoted to the big catering company in the sky, I reflected in amazement, it was good to know there was going to be someone in the new generation of canteen mums to take her place.

THE TRUTH ABOUT Lies

Little puffs of steam were wafting around the bathroom door and escaping into the hall. The shower was gushing full bore. 'Are you washing your hair?' I roared. 'Of course!' Rash bellowed over the torrent.

But he wasn't.

Of all the problems parenting presents, the truth about lying is the hardest to get across.

First there are the fantasy lies that adults tell children to bring them pleasure. Sometimes I wonder what they think when we stick to the story about all those brown chocolate eggs coming out of a fluffy white rabbit. Especially when I'm banning television for a week because they scoffed all the Mother's Day soft centres and then claimed that the dog ate them.

Do my children ever consider the story that a big man in a red suit delivers presents all over the world on Christmas Eve is a bit odd coming from the same woman who lectures them for an hour about the benefits of truthfulness after finding the chewable portion of their lunches (which they claimed to have eaten) in the kitchen bin?

With only their best interests at heart we tell our children that medicine will taste nice when it won't, that injections won't sting when in fact they sting like crazy, and that tests won't be hard when they almost always are.

We say their friends won't laugh at them — when they will. We tell them nightmares won't return — but they do. We explain that we will always know if they are telling a lie — but we don't.

Of course, in our family, Turbulence is the classic exception. Turb has always been so terrifyingly truthful that I have often yearned for a lie, just a little lie, any lie would do.

When I ask him after school if he has had a good day, how I long for him to lie, just once, and say 'yes, lovely, thanks', just to make me happy.

When the bullies backed him into a corner and demanded to know if it was Turb who dobbed them in for pelting rocks at the scripture teacher's station wagon, how I wish Turbulence had said: 'No, it was that big guy over there'.

How I pray for the day that I cry: 'Who broke the video recorder?' and Turbulence says: 'Not me' so that I don't have to punish the only member of my family who is willing to record my favourite shows so that I can watch them while I iron.

Serenity neither lies nor denies, nor does she ever admit guilt. Asked if she spilled cordial on the floor and failed to clean it up, she is always just on her way to get the wettex. Accused of taking Turb's possessions out of his hallowed room without asking, she is always just on her way to put them back. Expected to explain why she is two hours late coming home, she was always on her way but something (What? A flight to Melbourne? A board meeting? A nuclear test? What sort of vital issues delay a twelve-year-girl from walking two blocks to her front door?) just came up.

In the face of incontrovertible guilt she opens her eyes very wide and looks disbelieving, says nothing and quietly disappears.

Rash, of course, tells big lies. He goes to enormous lengths to construct and stage his mammoth untruths.

Hence, the shower. Having been told to wash his hair, he emerged with bone-dry locks. Sent back in to do the job properly, he turned the shower on hot and hard, dampened his hair with water from the basin tap and sat on the toilet reading a book for the time he judged it would normally have taken him to shampoo and condition. He then lied to me that the job was done.

Why? After all, in the time this complex operation took him, he could have washed his hair properly anyway!

In order to find an answer to Rash's perplexing behaviour, I looked up Lying in my notes for More Serious Stories.

It seems children lie: (1) To avoid punishment (but if he HAD washed his hair he would not have BEEN punished); (2) To get what they want (surely he didn't WANT to sit in a steamy bathroom reading?); (3) To win praise (No); (4) To protect themselves (From what? Since when has my approval ever been important to him?); (5) To avoid embarrassment (Rash is NEVER embarrassed); or (6) To demonstrate power.

Aaah. There it was. By pretending, but not washing his hair at all, Rash was demonstrating his power to defy me. Again.

There's only one thing to do. I'm working on a marvellous international disaster involving the tooth fairy, the Easter bunny, Santa Claus and a UFO.

When it comes to lies, he's about to find out he's up against the mother of them all!

SEX AND Violence

Bringing up your children to believe honestly and sincerely that we are all equal in every way is a difficult job. I know because I've failed.

I did my best. I bought Turbulence a pink skateboard, a mauve bike and fluorescent yellow laces for his sneakers. I taught him how to set the dial on the washing machine and make a packet cake. On birthdays I gave him dolls as well as cars, a tea set instead of a sword, and books in which the men wore aprons and the plumbers and astronauts were women.

The boy is tidy and sensitive, every liberated mother's dream. He puts away his Lego in colour-coded piles and files his socks. He unpacks the dishwasher without being asked, folds up his clothes, nurses babies and overflows like a blocked gutter when watching sad movies.

But as he and his Dad were doing the dishes last week, he asked us what a male chauvinist was.

'It's a bloke who believes that men are superior to women,' said his father.

Turbulence frowned and shrugged his shoulders beneath his pink T-shirt. 'But they are,' he said. 'Everyone knows that.'

'He can't help being sexist,' Serenity explained to me later as we were folding up her blue socks. 'He's stupid. All boys are stupid because they have smaller brains than us. Didn't you know?'

Like Turbulence, Serenity is full of contradictions with regard to the question of sexual equality. While she spends only a token minute or two on her hair and rarely wears pink, she spends hours of the school holidays painting her nails jangling cerise. She then pulls the sleeves of her huge jumpers over her fine and delicate hands so that they won't show.

She has devoted half her lifetime to perfecting the gorilla-like walk of the thirteen-year-old boy across the road. Despite years of mind-numbing physical culture and dancing classes, she walks with her shoulders slumped forward and her head hanging over her chest as if she is constantly searching for shreds of her lost femininity, which may have slipped down between the cracks in the pavement.

She can't decide whether to be a vet or an air hostess but she eventually plans to have 'one very small girl baby' so that the demands of motherhood won't impinge too far on her adult life.

Rash has read all the books and inherited all the unisex toys, including the coloured dolls and the pink plastic vacuum cleaner. He has also taken note of the fact that all the females and all the males in the household are bigger and smarter than him. As a result, he does not discriminate against either sex.

Instead, Rash, the smallest in our family by far, firmly believes that might is right.

A small warrior who is convinced that the strong shall inherit anything decent on this earth, he sneers at tears, thumbs his nose at pain and never wears a singlet. At two he was doing push ups, at three he taught himself karate. He is never without a weapon, sometimes imaginary, sometimes not.

To my shame Rash has the biggest collection of arms known to child. He has knives, swords, rifles, pistols, space guns, truncheons, bows and arrows. He attacks trees, animals, passing cars and imaginary bad guys but at my insistence, or should I say if I am around, he restricts himself to just shooting the kneecaps of living people.

To smaller boys, Rash is a hero. 'Is Rash playing with his GUNS?' his little cousin, Destructus, will ask me eagerly on the telephone. 'Actually,' I mumble nervously, 'he's just cuddling his teddy while I cut his toenails.' In fact, Rash is snapping his handcuffs onto his bear while he holds the manicure scissors to the unfortunate animal's throat.

Desty's Mum refuses to let him have weapons as toys and denies that when he points his drink bottle at Rash and says: 'Bang!' he's just doing what comes naturally.

On the other hand, I never bought a gun for Turbulence, and he never asked for one. Violence in any form terrified him. At playgroup he assumed responsibility for separating any babies who were silly enough to crawl into the same corner. Just watching people hug each other sent his adrenalin to record levels, because of the risk of them squeezing too tight. Which goes to show that nature and nurture are at war in even the most ordinary families.

At school, where weapons are banned, Rash and his vast circle of cool friends exchange frenzied cries, strike dazzling fighting poses and do terrifying karate kicks. Yet as far as I can work out, they never actually make body contact with each other.

Strangely, Rash's respect for strength has not made him macho. When he was four someone told him that Elizabeth II was the most important person in the Commonwealth. It was then that he publicly announced, to the considerable embarrassment of his family, that when he grew up he would like to be the Queen.

Every morning my two sons stand side by side before the bathroom mirror, Turbulence meditating on the superiority of the male as he wields the hair spray and Rash flexing his tiny ping pong ball muscles while practising some Very Serious Scowling.

At the school sports day as he stood briefly at my side, his hand on the hilt of his invisible sword and his trigger finger itching for action, we were approached by two plump, lumbering little boys.

'This is Ben,' said Rash. 'I call him Hippo. That's Li. I call him Bottomous. They're the best ones to chase.'

'Want to chase us now?' asked Hippo eagerly.

'Later, guys,' drawled Rash. 'I'll go after the fast ones first, while I'm feeling fit.'

My stomach turned over in horror. 'Why would you want to chase these nice boys?' I asked in despair.

All three boys looked at me in exasperation. 'Because they're slow,' Rash explained patiently. 'And they're soft to sit on when you catch them.'

He scowled and Hippo and Bottomous squealed and ran off. Slowly.

'Someone's got to do it,' said the warrior resignedly. And wielding a deadly school jacket, he ran into battle, leaving me to wait and weep, as all good women have done since the beginning of time.

TEACHER Talk

My little red moulded chair was so close to the ground that I couldn't find a place for my feet.

If I put them neatly together on the floor it meant my knees were level with my chin, which considerably reduced my dignity. But when I stretched my legs out in front of me they gave the impression that I was lounging, and lounging is not a recommended position outside a classroom.

The door was painted glossy green and in a small black box in its centre were printed the white letters 4J. Sitting in the tiny chair which encompassed only part of my bottom, I waited nervously for the door to open.

Schools, I reflected, are designed primarily for short people.

I ran through my opening lines, desperately searching for a tone which conveyed friendliness without familiarity, interest without neurosis, appreciation without gush, sweetness without sucking up. I knew nothing would work. My mouth was dry. My turn was next. I was about to go through the green door for the half-yearly parent-teacher interview.

Whether or not you dread parent-teacher interviews depends of course on the pupil concerned. I daresay if your child writes stories bursting with adjectival phrases, never messes up his mentals and has a bottom drawer overflowing with merit cards, you anticipate your interview with his teacher with the same sort of pleasure involved in looking forward to a delicious and satisfying meal.

Outside the green door I was suffering from stabbing stomach pains which resembled indigestion. Needless to say, I was there to talk about Rash.

But then, I've never been at my best during parent-teacher interviews, not even when Turbulence, Boy Who Did No Wrong, was the pupil in question.

The problem is that the children teachers deal with during the day, in the rule-ridden corridors of the school situation, are not the same people who live in the comparative chaos of their family homes.

Turbulence spent every night of his early school years in pain and anguish as he worried about the horrors that lay in store for him in both the classroom and the playground. I would huddle by his bed in the dark, trying desperately to suggest something pleasant in connection with school, failing, and making do by dabbing his eyes with tissues and reminding him that Christmas/Easter/his birthday/the holidays were only eleven months away.

Yet every morning he would present himself, neat, obedient and smiling, to teachers who soon realised that with Turbulence patrolling the playground with his rule book they could spend their playground duty in a picnic chair with a good novel.

Because few people were aware of the demons which played tunnel ball with his soul at night, Turbulence, a tidily average pupil, was a teacher's dream.

'Good Quiet Worker', his report cards read, 'Applies Himself Well', 'Lovely Manners' and of course, 'a Pleasure to Teach'. Was this the boy who cried himself to sleep at night because they'd moved the blackboard? Who hid in the toilet for forty-five minutes rather than stand in the back row of the choir on Open Day? Who needed a week off school because his imaginary friend's figment father had been transferred to Melbourne?

'It's quite normal for a little boy to occasionally get a bit upset,' said Miss Patience when he was in Year Three. 'Don't worry so much.'

'You don't understand,' I cried, starting to get more than a bit upset myself. 'He's always getting VERY upset.' In the end they made an appointment for me to see the student counsellor.

'Let me get this straight,' said Ms Doodle in the calm, slow tone that counsellors do so well. 'You say Turbulence always tidies his room without being asked? He puts his toys away?'

'In rows,' I answered helplessly, smelling the danger. 'And his clothes as well.'

She put her clipboard face-down on the desk, stood up and smoothed her thin skirt over her thick legs. 'This problem is too complex for me to handle,' she said. 'I'm not qualified to deal with your delusions. I will refer you to a psychiatrist.

'Meanwhile I don't think it's Turbulence who has the problem.'

Teachers have their own way of coping with ten-minute parent interviews; they are trained never to say anything too good or too bad. This meant that Serenity, Girl Who Excels, was more of a problem for them. 'Her work is of a quite High Standard,' said Miss Tips, when she topped Year One. 'Her untidy handwriting spoils an otherwise Good Effort,' said Miss Foible when she earned straight As in Year Three. 'Shows Promise', commented Mr Fusst, handing over her annual highest achievement award in Year Five. What did she have to do, I wondered, for one of them to admit to me that she was smart?

Conversely, Rash's academic progress at school also leaves his teachers struggling for an appropriate comment. So far it's been suggested that, apart from giving me a break, school for our youngest child is a total waste of time.

But when the Green Door opened I found myself face to face with the legendary Miss Match, who is reputed to be to education what sauce is to sausages.

Instead of sitting at attention behind her desk she was perched on its corner, inhaling deeply from a yellow musk stick.

'First, you'd better take these home,' she said, jerking her thumb at an enormous carton, which bulged with weapons, the results of six months' confiscations.

'Rash is a great kid,' she grinned, offering me a musk stick from a crumbled white packet and groping for a match. 'Everybody likes him. He loves to have a go. He's a card. He's a clown. He's a real boy's boy.'

I reminded her it was Rash Storm we were talking about. 'Short boy. Talks a lot. Usually heavily armed.'

'That's the one,' she said. 'He makes my day.'

'You're not telling me he's a Pleasure to Teach?'

'Yep.'

'You're not going to say Improvement Needed. Or that he Could Try Harder?'

'He couldn't,' she said. 'He's too busy being a kid.'

I told her I wasn't qualified to deal with her delusions and went sadly away.

I wondered how long it would be before he had Miss Match back on real cigarettes.

A LOT OF SOMETHING Extra

It was a long, drawn-out affair and we were all weary by the end of it. Most of us emerged a little sadder, a little wiser, a little older, a little wetter, a little poorer — and I, for one, emerged with a head full of straight greying hair!

I refer of course to the first term of the school year.

For the Storm family, term one finally brought to a head the exhausting and emotive issue of extracurricular activities.

The crisis was sparked off by Rash turning eight. As most parents know, this is the age at which children leave behind their voluminous uniforms, their colour-coordinated backpacks and their manners, and enter primary school, with all the nasty side effects this entails. These include refusing to wear the correct uniform, speaking without moving their lips and dragging their graffiti-covered barrel bags through every gutter between school and home.

However, at the age of eight, our children also become eligible for every extracurricular activity known to man. And Rash, popular, perverse and always armed to the teeth, chose to do them all.

With the wisdom of hindsight, I have had a reasonably easy time with extracurriculars to date. It was only peer pressure (mine) which finally forced Turbulence away from his ninety-nine jigsaw puzzles and propelled him into swimming (which made him cold), soccer (which gave him a headache) and Boys Brigade (which he enjoyed as long as the scripture stories had a happy ending). We tried piano but he worried that the black notes were not evenly distributed along the keyboard.

Serenity, Girl Who Excels, dabbled in dancing, picked at the piano, stalked through physical culture and fiddled with the flute, but after winning a drawer full of awards, settled comfortably into Brownies, music lessons and swimming once a week. Somehow we escaped netball.

In fact, her passion for art and craft badges turned her into the most dedicated Brownie who ever made a promise, and we were concerned that she was in danger of being the oldest Brownie in the western world. She was certainly the tallest and when she reached the stage where she towered a good three inches over Lowanna (roughly translated from Dreamtime lingo into Laid Back Leader of Lots of Little Girls) she had to hang up her mushroom.

After being dragged around to his siblings' activities for eight years, with swimming lessons his only release, Rash threw himself into the new year with an enthusiasm normally reserved for adding to his weapon collection.

By Valentine's Day, Rash was 'doing' cubs, swimming squad, tennis, Little Athletics, piano lessons and French language classes. He was also allowed to attend school discos, although they disarmed him at the door.

By St Patrick's Day he had also started soccer, Sunday School, basketball and karate. While he thoroughly enjoyed them all, he was churlish and cheeky at home, partly because this was the required attitude for primary school and partly because he never got to bed before nine.

I became frantic. I was getting RSI from signing the cheques for his fees. I seemed to be permanently pumping petrol. The washing hung listlessly on the line for days, waiting for me to be home from Rash's activities long enough to bring it in.

I never was.

Worse, I could never find the time or the finance for my beginning-of-the-year perm and colour rinse, a necessary rejuvenation measure after every school holiday.

'Something's got to go,' I groaned. 'You choose.' But he couldn't. He needed karate for his arm muscles and running for his legs and swimming for his lungs and French for his future. How could he give up cubs when the leaders actually said (out loud) that boys should be allowed to be boys? Playing the piano was a guarantee of stardom and as for soccer — the guys couldn't do without his incredible ball skills.

Rash doesn't have a self-esteem problem.

I gave him until the end of the week to make a decision. My hair turned another shade lighter, my wallet became thinner. Then, on the Friday night, he arrived home carrying an enormous case and wearing an even more enormous grin.

'I've decided to give up tennis, basketball and French,' he said, 'because they're on the same three nights that the school band practises. They had auditions today, and I had more air than anyone else in Year Three.'

As panic ricocheted around my heart, Rash produced from its case, the school's trumpet.

'You don't have to pay anything for a while,' he soothed me as I tried to fit my greying head into the microwave. 'They said you could just think about it while I looked after it over the weekend.'

'Is it a trumpet?' I asked bitterly. 'Or a guinea pig?'

But I lifted the phone to cancel my perm, and as his first ghastly blast filled the family room, my dream of crisp brown curls withered and died.

'It could be worse,' said Turbulence sympathetically. 'You'd have to feed a guinea pig. Anyway, he might get to be good at it.'

'Or he'll get sick of it,' said Serenity, 'and he'll probably never practise.'

They were both wrong.

CAMP Malinger

When you are face to face with a well-groomed woman in her fifties wearing matte make-up, a perfect perm and expensive shoes and she wants you to call her Balloo the Bear, it's hard to feel comfortable.

After all, there's nothing about her immaculate shirt and her newly pressed culottes which reminds you even remotely of a large hairy creature which beats its breast and shakes tree trunks.

And besides, you've been used to calling her Betty.

There's probably a simple explanation why cub leaders are named after Rudyard Kipling's storybook animals. But Rash isn't in cubs for folklore or facts. He's in it, pure and simple, for fun. And Betty, sorry, Balloo, makes the fun happen.

Personally, I don't find camping fun. I like clean sheets, flushing loos and posturepaedics. The sound of birdsong gives me a headache. When I hear a kookaburra laugh, I never get the joke.

What was I doing at Camp Malinger? When Rash joined the cubs I had been prepared to sew on batteries of badges, but I had expected his father to be the one who would be joining him for dust and damper in the bush.

The answer of course, is Balloo.

I was here because of the calm Max Factor smile the Bear gave me when she said: 'Your son has joined us just in time for the mother and son camp. We have dear little cabins and it's fully catered for, so all the mums have to do is have fun with their boys.' I was here because if she wanted to, Balloo could sell honey to bears.

As it turned out, the night before 22 cubs and 21 mothers (who WAS that sensible woman?) descended on the creaking, wafer-thin huts of Camp Malinger, the caretaker/cook and his wife packed up their pots and left in a fit of pique.

With Balloo, her angular husband, Kaa, the Python and Bagheera, the Panther (. . . actually a small, pretty mother with carefully applied blusher and pierced ears), we began our weekend of fun in the kitchen. With our sleeves rolled back we swept up possum droppings and scoured the sinks, just in case something a little warmer than rain had fallen into them overnight.

Then Kaa left with the cubs to lay a nature trail for the Mums to follow. Unfortunately as none of us were familiar with cubs' bush lore and as the Bear and the Panther had been forced to remain back at Malinger whipping up lunch for 40, we walked through the carefully arranged arrows of pebbles, tripped on the signs constructed out of twigs and ignored the paper messages clinging precariously to the gums.

We talked a lot and laughed and after a while as the track disappeared we laughed less and wheezed more. Eventually, when the thorns and vines became thick and wild and the hills turned into sheer cliffs with only one foothold to share between us all, we began to pant and I'm sorry to say it, to swear. Some of us may even have wept.

Just as we seemed to be on the outskirts of Darwin, Kaa and the biggest cubs came crashing through the undergrowth to rescue us. They made no attempt to hide their scorn and chastened, we struggled back to camp, where the younger cubs had eaten all the hamburgers.

I had not envisaged going out again after lunch, with a small group of bruised and weary women, and wandering soggily about in the rain with a bundle of tent pegs, some fishing line and a compass. It was Kaa's idea. Apparently we were making a drawing with fishing line in the grass.

A long time later it turned out to be a ship. Kaa was proud of us. He told us so. We looked at him strangely .

Later, while the wind howled and the cubs shrieked, we lay in the dark on our anorexic mattresses, thinking of our husbands far away with the electric blankets all to themselves. We thought of Balloo's 'lovely little huts'. We thought of Kaa being proud of us.

And all through that wild and stormy night we were kept awake by our plans for revenge.

But in the morning, with our hair in clumps and our eyes red raw, we meekly held out our plates for more. An immaculate Balloo and Bagheera, who had both been up for hours, loaded bacon on to them. We sighed and followed the fresh possum droppings to our tables. Our boys were full of laughter, cheek and fried eggs, and ready to get going. Obediently we washed up, swept, scrubbed and then consulted our compasses for the next hike. We even managed to nod eagerly when Balloo asked us if we were having fun.

How, we wondered, had Balloo managed to convince us all that we should smile and Do Our Best?

Obviously, it's not easy to say no to a bear.

Especially a Bear as nice as Betty.

FORGETTING TO Remember

Question: What is big and black and shiny and should be in the music room at school?

Answer: Rash's trumpet case, the one which is standing in the middle of the hall, one metre from the front door, waiting for Rash to collect it on his way out so that he will be properly equipped for band practice today.

The only trouble is that Rash left for school an hour ago and now I am faced with one of the most daunting decisions known to parents all over the western world.

Should I take his trumpet to the school, saving him from disgrace, inconvenience and embarrassment? Or should I leave it at home, teaching him the folly of his forgetfulness?

According to all the child psychologists, to rescue my son from this latest attack of chronic absentmindedness will only make his disease worse. He must learn from his experience. To put it more strongly, he must suffer in order to be cured.

But how much suffering will Rash actually experience? He won't have his trumpet, therefore he will not be able to attend band practice. Instead, he will probably play handball in the quadrangle or chase the girls in the grass area behind the toilet block. As he thoroughly enjoys both these activities, he is not likely to experience much anguish over the loss of an hour's hard blowing.

It's me who would incur the greatest loss, in the form of an hour's tuition fees written off in the interests of teaching Rash a lesson.

I once tried not taking him his lunch when he forgot it. He borrowed money from the teacher and ended up with chicken nuggets and flavoured milk, a much more exciting lunch than the peanut butter sandwich which lolled limply in its Gladwrap at home.

I tried not taking Rash's hat when he forgot it. 'No hat, no play' is the firm rule at his school. So he went to the library and volunteered to operate the computer, guaranteeing him not only an hour of electronic fun and games, but a merit card from the librarian for his 'citizenship'.

I tried not taking Rash's jacket when he forgot it. He caught a cold and enjoyed three days off school watching television while I spent a fortune on antibiotics and inhalers, endured tides of incoming germs in the doctor's surgery and lay awake all night listening to him cough.

I tried not taking Rash's medicine to school when he forgot it. He got better.

Last but not least, I refused to take his homework to school when he left it on the kitchen bench. For this he definitely suffered. The absence of a homework star that day left Rash ineligible for the mother of all merit awards, the Great Golden.

He said he would have remembered his book if only SOMEONE hadn't double parked the toaster in front of it. In vain I cried out that the toast was for his breakfast, not mine. Everyone Else's Mother, he remarked, remembered not to forget to remind their children to remember.

My guilt was overwhelming.

But hey, what if I wasn't here? What if I was at work all day, as so many mums are? If I worked in an office, rather than in my own house, I would be unable to see the trumpet case. I wouldn't be worrying about whether or not to take it to him. It simply would not be possible.

The answer to that is that I'm NOT in an office. I'm at home, staring at the trumpet case in the hall.

But I DO have work to do. And if I go up to the school I will have to change my clothes and colour in my lips and risk running into the nice lady in the office whose daughter has just had her first baby. My day is simply not long enough for a conversation with this woman.

Besides, she will say: 'Hullo Mrs Storm. What have your children forgotten today?' And I will have to pretend that I'm amused.

Another thought has just struck me. If Rash misses out on an hour's trumpet practice at school, he might decide to do it at home instead.

At last I know what I have to do. I've read the books. I've heard the experts. I must find the strength and the courage to give up this futile rescuing behaviour. And I will.

But before I start I'll just pop up to the school with the trumpet.

PROJECTS: THE TEACHERS' Revenge

I saw the smug grin of triumph spread across the woman's face as she opened her son's project book and I guessed the reason why. She was still standing at the school gate; she didn't even have the decency to wait until she was back in her car.

I knew she must have been given an A+ for her project on Japan!

How unfair! It was only because they could afford encyclopaedias AND her husband worked in the travel industry, with access to all those brochures. I'd never once seen her in the library, red-eyed and ratty like the rest of us.

She giggled with relief and happiness as she and her child waltzed away. A thirty-five-year-old who giggles, I thought in disgust. She must have the mentality of a child.

My mark was a mediocre B– despite the hours I'd spent in the library, on the phone, on my knees sorting and cutting pictures, up to my elbows in glue. But I knew where I'd gone wrong. It was the margins. I'd let Serenity rule them up herself. And the shading. Serenity's colouring-in is okay but it takes an expert to shade around all those islands.

Sometimes when I'm still awake at midnight, tying the final piece of string to a model of the solar system or printing the last captions beneath grubby samples of raw and manufactured Australian wool, I wonder idly what malevolent being in the Department of School Education first introduced the idea of doing school projects into our society. Surely a concept so time-consuming, so frustrating, so threatening to family relationships, so universally despised by both parents and pupils alike — and so unutterably futile — could not have come from the brain of a normal human being?

Projects are the teachers' revenge. They are the means teachers use to get back at us for leaving our children with them for six hours a day, five days a week, often without a word of appreciation other than an anorexic hand towel and a can of smelly talc at Christmas.

Teachers know perfectly well that children can never do their own projects. They don't have the ability, the authority, the means of transport, the finance or the experience to get the information. So it's up to the parents, who have all of the above, to help. As a result, projects keep parents poor, pressured, paranoid and up all night.

I know schools have to set homework. I can put up with hearing the kids' spelling while I mash the potatoes and I'll chant a table or two with them as long as we don't have to do it to the tune of that song out of the *Lion King*. I don't even mind the occasional science experiment as long as it's not the one with the seeds in the cotton wool which has never, in three generations, produced a single little green sprout for me or for anyone related to me. (It's genetic — we have the same effect on African violets.)

But projects! I hate everything about them. I hate the way the sheets of cardboard curl at the corners even before the first husk of wheat is stapled onto them. By the time you have cut a lump of lining from your ugh boot for a wool sample, something has been spilled on the captions and your child's single contribution — the fancy lettering — is running into trouble as it merges with the Clag.

I hate the way the project books from the newsagent are cunningly and cruelly designed never to have enough pages. Attaching a new book which remains half empty indicates that you haven't done enough research. Cramming it all into one will lose you marks for messy presentation and hence, poor parent participation. The only alternative is to stay up all night looking for more pictures of the Murrumbidgee Irrigation Area or Australian mammals or life on the Tigris-Euphrates or The Sphinx, to fill them up.

I hate the way the librarians look disapproving while you tell them what you need and then make a point of showing your child, rather than you, where to find it. The child nods seriously, walks to the indicated shelf and then . . . hey! There's Ben! Or Benita! And the kids talk animatedly about cricket or gym while you and Ben's mum crouch on your haunches, rifling through the shelves at a rapid rate, trying to remember the new name for the new capital of China and wondering if you turned off the heat under the potatoes before you left.

I hate the way the children sulk and whine when you make them come inside out of the sun on Saturdays so you can sit beside them circling slabs of information or trying to find something that isn't relevant only to America on the computer encyclopaedia which cost you more than your washing machine but doesn't realise there's a Great South Land.

I become unreasonably irritated when their eyes glaze over while I am trying so hard to make it easy. I get tense after spending hours summarising all the available information on a Day in the Life of a Young Mediaeval Soldier, only to return to their room after an hour and a half to discover that all they've written so far is: 'A typical Young Mediaeval Soldier would rise at dawn.'

I hate the way projects make you wish you'd never had children.

After all the tears and anxiety which accompanied every project Turbulence attempted, and realising I had two more children to drag through the project nightmare, I decided to prepare myself for the future by keeping a well stocked project box. Over the years I have filled this box with every magazine and newspaper lift-out, *National Geographic*, educational calendar, postcard, travel book, pamphlet and project supplement that has come my way. I have stocked it with pieces of greasy wool, balls of raw cotton, shells, lizard skeletons, fur, strange rocks, seed pods, photographs, shells and unidentified lumps of colourful matter from the garden.

Not once in the history of my three children's school careers has anything in that box been required.

I thought the worst project I had ever tackled was Serenity's Life Cycle of a Mosquito (with photographs of the highlights!) until Turbulence started high school and came home with an assignment entitled: 'Livestock Breeds: A report on the past, present and future of Australia's sheep, cattle, goat, pig and poultry industries.'

My stomach heaved when I read the first of 60 questions. I closed my eyes. 'Turbulence,' I croaked. 'You're on your own.'

Somehow he got through it without my help. Although just between you and me, his Drawing of a Well-Hung Bull left a lot to be desired.

IN FOR Repairs

Even if children were born with a warranty, ours would doubtless have expired by now. What rotten luck. Having provided me with two relatively fault-free models, Mother Nature has played a nasty trick . . . she obviously designed my children to function correctly only for the first ten years.

Of course in the perverse way first-born children have of rolling off the assembly line and immediately tipping the world as we know it upside down, Turbulence did not break down in the way you would expect.

Indeed, it's still hard to believe that he managed to snap his carefully nurtured arm in two at all.

Is this the boy who still prefers to play cricket with a sponge rubber ball? Who withdrew from the football team after checking the texture of the grass on the try line? Who wouldn't complete his Lego models until his chipped nail mended? Who spends his pocket money on dandruff shampoo? Who wears kneepads when watching television in case he falls off the couch?

In fact, Turbulence broke his arm while watching his father dig a hole for our above-ground swimming pool. (Don't ask.) Other people's sons rush in with shovels to help with such important men's work, but not the Storm son. Turbulence was watching. And as he watched, he slipped. He fell down gently on his bottom and somehow or other, his arm snapped.

Of course, we didn't believe him.

He hugged his arm and I ran my eye over his denim jacket to check for grass stains.

A couple of hours later I found him sitting on the couch, keeping very still. His eyes were red. Naturally, as it was a Sunday night, I assumed he was having his weekly anxiety crisis. I gave him an aspirin and he went to bed.

The next morning he asked for another painkiller. I wondered if he was becoming an addict. But he went off to school without a fuss. (That alone should have alerted my attention.)

Late that afternoon, when he yelped unusually loudly after bumping into Rash's kicking foot, I finally looked beneath his sleeve.

The guilt was unbelievable.

I have never had a broken bone. I thought broken limbs caused excruciating agony and the sort of screaming anguish which was demonstrated by Douglas Portly, a little boy in my kindergarten class at Blister Road Primary, who fell out of a tree while trying to see into the female teachers' toilet.

I raced Turbulence to the Medical Centre where a curly-headed Indian doctor in a neat knitted vest confirmed my awful suspicions. 'Broken, isn't it?' he smiled. 'You should have come much sooner.'

It would have been different if Turbulence had suddenly come down with an asthma attack. Our third child, Rash, the one who did not come fault-free (I suppose by the time you get to number three some of the production machinery has rusted up a little) inherited my asthma. As a result, I know every variety of wheeze and cough, I can read breath the way other people read palms, my cupboards are bulging with spinhalers, inhalers and enormous boxes of capsules designed to bring back breath and I know what it's like to read *The Muddle Headed Wombat* aloud at three a.m., after countless sleepless nights, with the same exhausted lack of expression my mother used when she read it to me.

I'm also pretty good with colds.

I would have recognised a cold or an asthma attack. But I didn't even have a nodding acquaintance with a broken arm.

I didn't realise it meant a return to full-time mother care, from washing the hair to doing up buttons to cutting up meat. I didn't foresee a bathroom and bedroom full of unusual contraptions made from plastic bags, rubber bands, coat hangers and rope, all designed to allow Turbulence to look after himself and his arm as modestly and autonomously as he could manage.

And until Serenity tried to insert herself between the telephone receiver and me the other day, in order to tell me that her arm was sore, I didn't realise it could happen twice in the same family.

'I fell off my bike,' said Serenity, who suffers enthusiastically from everything she can think of at any given moment.

I rolled my eyes, reached for the fridge and pulled out a packet of frozen peas. Still talking on the telephone (Rash's extracurricular activities take a good deal of coordination) I tossed them to her. 'Stick that on it for a minute,' I hissed.

But experience sent a small warning buzz to my brain. When I noticed the red lining around her eyes an hour later, I decided to postpone the search for Rash's sneaker until we had made a trip to the Medical Centre.

'Aha!' said the same curly-headed doctor, wearing the same knitted vest. 'So you have decided to make this an annual event?'

Serenity's arm wasn't snapped, it was lumped. A greenstick fracture. 'There's no need for me to tell you what to do, is there?' said the doctor as he checked the cast.

I said there wasn't. The guilt was formidable. But the prospect of dressing and washing Serenity for four long weeks, of cutting up her meat and washing her hair and doing up her laces and being forced to express sympathy while she limply lapped it up, was punishment enough.

I decided that after I had treated myself to a mild asthma attack I would ring my obstetrician and demand my money back.

DOING Without

'**The worst thing about children,' said my visitor, 'is that** they never know when to stop. No matter how much they get, they always ask for more.'

'Like Oliver Twist?' I asked politely, offering her my best silver tray and watching her take another Tim Tam.

'Yes, although at least he was at boarding school,' said my friend, licking a beautifully manicured finger. 'Boarding school is the best place for children, don't you think? Not that I would know, of course, as I don't have kids.'

Why wasn't I surprised?

You could tell at first glance that our visitor was a VC — one of society's Voluntarily Childless. It would have been obvious to any parent — after all, she was wearing white, her skin was smooth and unlined and her handbag was flat. It was also clear from the way she flinched when Turbulence, Serenity and Rash fell through the screen door in a heap of limbs and curls and perspiration, and asked noisily if the chocolate biscuits were for them as well.

'Those who ask don't get,' said my visitor, smiling at them sweetly and smoothing her white linen slacks over thighs which had never been bashed about by childbirth. 'That's what my mother always said when we were greedy.'

'What MY mother always says,' said Turbulence earnestly, 'is that we should remind her about afternoon tea early so we're not eating too close to dinner time.'

Some Voluntarily Childless people are sensible career women who are banging their brilliantly hard heads on glass ceilings. Some are car crazy, some are wise world travellers and some are as silly as sausages. But VCs all have one thing in common. While confessing frankly that they know nothing about bringing up children, none of them can resist having a little go at it when the opportunity presents itself.

'Can't the children do their own packing?' she asked disapprovingly as we prepared to celebrate our reunion by taking her away for a long weekend at the beach. 'Surely it's just a matter of folding some shorts and T-shirts and grabbing their toothbrushes?'

I thought of explaining Serenity's tendency, when preparing for a journey, to tip her top drawer into her backpack and consider herself ready to roll. I could have mentioned Turbulence's horror of having to be parted from any of his possessions at all — including all his tapes and Lego and the collection of felt footballs he sewed and stuffed in kindergarten. I baulked at telling her that whenever Rash prepared for a trip all he packed were his pyjama bottoms and his weapons.

I had trouble explaining the cereals and spreads that had to be crammed into the food carton, and why we were taking the games box, the five sets of sheets, the medication bag, the books — and the towels! It was clear to me that my friend had never been anywhere at all where a towel was not provided.

During her two-week stay my friend did her best to adapt. She showed Serenity how to braid her hair and said she smelled nice. She was jubilant when Turbulence let her beat him at chess. She coped with the shock of watching me do five loads of washing on Mondays and she forgave me for serving spaghetti bolognaise twice in ten days.

But Rash was beyond her perimeters of tolerance. She continually asked why we let him bat for so long at cricket, why he was allowed to join us for ice cream when he hadn't eaten his greens and why, when he had worn us out, he was allowed to watch television. She couldn't understand why he had to be so heavily armed, how he became so dirty so fast and how he could make so much noise. In fact, she was loudly mystified as to why we let him inside the house at all.

At her farewell party, at my request, Rash put on his best clothes and sacrificed the role of warrior for that of waiter. Beaming cleanly in a bow tie, he served dip and biscuits to our mutual friends. He was careful, polite and patient and he didn't drop a crumb.

Towards the end of the evening he offered our guest of honour a final Tim Tam.

'I'd like to but I won't,' said the VC. 'I don't want to set Rashy a bad example, now that he's finally lost his guns and found where his MANNERS were hiding.'

Holding the silver dish aloft, Rash slid his free hand inside his smart little waistcoat and then drew his hand back out again with his fingers arranged in the shape of a pistol. He cocked it with his thumb and raised the imaginary barrel to the VC's pearly throat.

'Make my day, shweetheart,' he snarled softly. 'Have another biscuit.'

To a chorus of titters she opened her mouth to speak, changed her mind, turned prettily pink and took two. Rash made no further comment. He quietly put his fingers back inside his waistcoat and turned his weapon into a harmless hand.

Unlike my visitor, Rash knew when to stop.

VILLAIN WANTED:
BYO Ears

Once upon a time, when I was a little girl, there was nothing more exciting than getting dressed up in our Sunday School frocks and our black patent leather shoes, and going into the city to see a Christmas pantomime.

Those were the days of vast glittering casts, when the heroes wore tights and tap shoes, the heroines had enormous vowel sounds and the stage was filled with rows of sequinned girls and boys in satin strides.

But the real star of every pantomime was the evil villain — lecherous, leering, cackling, cunning and cruel. Terrifying. Bent on destruction. Wicked to the end. In fact, really BAD.

What I want to know is, where have all the baddies gone?

Like cooking, show business has become much more comfortable and convenient than it used to be. Our kids don't have to get dressed up or go further than their local shopping centre to see a panto or Christmas show. But why must the villains be comfortable too? Why have the beasts in these shows become so mild, so feeble, so eager to please?

Perhaps the producers believe our kids need some light relief from the horrors, both manufactured and real, that are blasted at them from their film and television screens.

But is it just me? Or is there something disappointing about a show from which all the evil and menace has been siphoned, along with scenery, props and much of the original plot?

I know the big budget stuff is beyond the producers' pockets these days. But frankly, there's something about watching a wicked wolf putting on his make-up which kills the thrill of terror you expect from a snarling carnivore.

Even the little girls whose mothers still make them wear dresses failed to be frightened of the wolf who starred with Red Riding Hood in this year's holiday pantomime at Treestump South community centre.

There was no woodchopper. Far from being sliced into bite-size fillets with an axe, the wolf apologised and stayed for decaffeinated tea at Granny's cottage.

The scariest part of the show was that Granny didn't live in a Safety House!

I thought they'd gone too far last year when they put on Snow White and the Two Dwarves. (You knew which one was Snow White because she wore a hair band instead of a beanie.) They dispensed with the witch altogether and made do with a mirror on the wall and a prerecorded message.

This year they kept the villain but eliminated the evil. We were asked to watch while the cast of three painted their faces and dressed for their parts. The wolf wore a green velvet smoking jacket and donned a magnificent tail. He waved, minced about the stage, and smiled a good deal at the audience, reassuring them that he was still simply a youth with a skin problem DRESSED as a wolf, and not a really truly terrifying wolf at all.

I'm sure the audience would have preferred a snarling monster. I KNOW they would have preferred a wolf with some sort of ears. We were all worried about what would happen when we got to Little Red's tactless comment about their size.

I was uncomfortable watching the grandmother construct her own cupboard out of a cardboard carton. I was embarrassed that a woman of her supposedly advanced years was wearing rubber sneakers with synthetic uppers. I didn't want to see the wolf flossing his deadly fangs.

Kids LIKE being temporarily terrified. Even Turbulence, our most fearful child, used to welcome the chance to be scared stiff of a slavering beast, with a taste for blond girls or pigs, who would be satisfactorily killed off at the end of the production. It was only the evil real-life nasties, such as the Possibility of an

Accident, or Getting Lost or Mummy Not Being There which prevented him from sleeping at night.

I remember a story about a little boy who was so bored during a modern production of Sleeping Beauty that he called out to the Wicked Fairy: 'You'll find her up in the tower with the spinning wheel!'

These holidays Rash felt the same way. Realising that the simpering wolf didn't have a chance against the two fast-talking Hood women, he ran down to the edge of the stage and offered the wolf his current favourite weapon — a plastic sword which accompanies him everywhere.

'You might have a chance with this,' said Rash politely. When the wolf laughed and pushed the sword away, my son returned with a shrug. 'What can you expect from a wolf with no ears?' he muttered. 'He didn't hear a word I said.'

GETTING Picky

My niece, Demanda, has been chosen as Rebecca Rabbit for the Easter play. Her mother is cutting up her favourite ugh boots for the ears and she's going to wear a blue bow around her neck to prove that she doesn't come from a sexist family.

Try as I might, I can't prevent the evil tendrils of envy from curling around my wicked heart and squeezing it tight. Why is Demanda being allowed to grab the spotlight as Rebecca Rabbit when at Treestump South Public, Rash has once again missed out on a starring role and has been cast as a bush?

Why should Demanda monopolise the spotlight in her sheepskin ears and cotton wool tail when Turbulence, my first-born son, the light of my loins, has never worn anything more spectacular on stage than his grey school uniform and a smile sticker? And even that wasn't for talent. It was his reward for being the only boy in kindergarten who sat still.

It's a sad fact of life that neither of my sons seems destined to be picked for something special on the school stage.

Every Monday morning of his primary school career, Turbulence sat up so straight when they read out the merit cards at assembly that when he got home we sometimes had to soak him in the bath for an hour before pliability returned to his rigid spine. But his name was never called.

As he didn't even have a nodding acquaintance with a bat and ball and didn't like to swim or run too fast in case he got puffed, he was never eligible for a sports award. As for drama, he found real life far too full of that sort of thing to have to act; no teacher ever dared to ask him to try.

One year he gave up every single lunch time to help the school gardener. We breathed a sigh of relief when speech day came around as we knew this grubby sacrifice automatically qualified Turbulence for a citizenship award which he would at last ascend the giddy heights of the school hall stage to receive.

We were wrong. For the first time that year they invited the gardener to personally bestow the certificates. He chose to do it the day before the prize giving, in his tool shed.

In kindergarten, Rash was cast as Joseph in the Christmas nativity. It was a non-speaking role but it was a start. Since then he has been trying too hard to make a comeback. At his teacher's insistence, he sits in the front row at school, so she can keep an eye on his creativity, and whether she's choosing a marching leader, a good reader, a band conductor, a class captain or the star of the next class play, Rash's thrusting hand, punching the air with powerful enthusiasm, is just too close for comfort.

Perhaps she can't focus on the front row. Or perhaps she remembers the day when she was standing by his desk and Rash threw up his hand so fast that it came into sudden sharp contact with her nose. Fame and recognition have eluded him ever since. (I refer of course, only to his stage career. In the normal run of life, Rash and his weapon collection are recognised everywhere we go.)

In an effort to experience the limelight, Turbulence and Rash used to hold their own concerts on our back veranda. They hooked their tennis racquets to large cardboard cartons and played them very loudly indeed while John Smith and the Right Notes blared from the ghetto blaster. Frequently Rash leapt down into the hordes of screaming fans and crowd-surfed between numbers but Turbulence stayed on the stage, concerned that close contact with the audience might make him claustrophobic.

These concerts were wonderful while the fans were fictional. I began to worry when I was at the shops one day and my friend Moana tapped me on the shoulder and said she would see me on Sunday. She had bought a ticket to Turb's Rock Concert. I went home and tried to book a seat too but all the chairs were sold out and I could only get a place on the rug for ten cents. I thought the price was a bit exorbitant seeing I was the one who had to wash it the next day.

The irony of course, is that Serenity, who couldn't care less whether she is chosen for anything, always gets picked.

While Turbulence brought home his single merit certificate and encased it forever in a gold frame, Serenity's merit cards rioted and reproduced in piles in the bottom of her school bag. They remained there for weeks until it was time to sort them out from the stickers and orange peel and present them in multiples of ten in order to receive the king-sized version. On stage of course.

Serenity was the fairy on the Christmas tree in kindergarten and the narrating angel in first class, the Pied Piper who led the Book Week Parade in Year Three, and Mary in the Year Five Nativity. If she stayed on her knees, she and Joseph were the same height. She conducted the school band, carried the flag in the Anzac Day service and was elected class captain three times. Not that she cared.

Only in Year Two did she appear to miss out. She was simply cast as one of the Easter daisies. When I made the mistake of joking about this to her teacher, the woman looked at me coldly and told me I was misinformed. 'Serenity is the HEAD of the Easter daisies,' she said. 'She shows the other daisies how to grow. She's the only flower in the play with a speaking part.'

And now Demanda is following in her big cousin's footsteps with another starring role. While outside my kitchen window, Rash has tied his own feet together and is standing very still with his arms raised high in the air. In each hand he holds a fan of plastic knives and swords.

He's practising being a bush.

THE DEAD PRESENTS Society

We had to move house this year because we needed five bedrooms . . . one for each of our sons, Turbulence and Rash, one for our daughter Serenity, one for us and one for dead presents.

For a fleeting instant on the day we packed the toys into the tea chests, I entertained the idea of taking them all to the tip instead. But the children, seeing them, flung themselves on to their old, forgotten treasures with the same mindless enthusiasm which they bestow on them every year on Christmas Eve, when they see me packing them up to donate to the St Vincent de Paul Society.

'You can't give THAT away; it's my favourite' ranks with 'everyone else has got one' and 'Mum, guess what Santa's bringing ME this Christmas?' as the phrases most likely to drive the parents of the western world into deep debt and despair.

Mums and dads who have been there and done that tell you about contractions, sleepless nights, toilet training and sexism but they never tell you about STORAGE.

Weeks before Christmas every year, the shops are already overloaded with stacks of toys which will almost certainly have a life span of one or two weeks, after which they will be left to meet their neglected end in toy boxes, cupboards and garages all over the city.

Take table tennis or ping pong tables, for example. Well you can't take them anywhere of course and they are far too large to store, except in the garage — and the inconvenient aspect of garages is that most people want to keep cars in them.

Every year hundreds of parents invest not only in ping pong tables but in extensions to their family rooms, in which to house their ping pong tables. They build new garages, extend carports, erect covered pergolas made of fancy tin and green webbing, they buy racks of bats and second refrigerators to hold drinks for the fevered ping pong players.

Ping pong tables are always a smash hit on Christmas Day when the uncles and dads join with the kids in Family Fun, not to mention Family Cheating and Family Fights when the owners of the table can't get near it.

By Boxing Day the average ping pong table is well on its way to becoming obsolete. Sticky cordial patterns run along the green squares, squashed insects cling to its corners. Few last till New Year's. If the thing is still on four legs by Australia Day, you're lucky. By Easter it is permanently propped on its side, because of the space it takes up in the shed/sleepout/extension/yard. By the following Christmas, it's a dead present.

Toddler pools have a short life. The type with tubes for walls are quickly punctured, the blue ones on metal frames bend and snap when children dive from them (what else can you do in eight inches of water but practise your diving?), the ones with walls held up by the force of water take so long to fill that by the time the walls are vertical, winter has arrived.

Old, punctured pools are impossible to stack or store. They kill the grass beneath them, visitors trip over their rusting frames. Glossy blue and orange in the department store displays, two weeks after Christmas they are faded, cracked and crying out for water as they lie parched and pitiful, dying of thirst in back yards where hoses are always around the front.

Hundreds of plastic bats, currently in pairs on the shop shelves, will soon be separated forever, all to die of loneliness because on the rare occasion that two children simultaneously feel like bashing a sponge ball back and forth, the second bat will never be found.

Rabbits, robots, monkeys, remote control cars, speedboats and trains will run down and choke on their own acid as parents everywhere will continually forget to replace the batteries.

By far the most space-consuming presents are boxes of track. If it wasn't for his track collection, and his rubber boat, Turbulence might almost have fitted his bed into his new room.

There are figure of eight tracks, loop the loops, train tracks, wooden, metal and plastic tracks, tracks with snazzy little cars and motorbikes and trains to whizz around them.

All tracks are designed to function in vast, unfurnished rooms in which there is no carpet and where the floor is durable and dust free. As not every suburban home has such a room, the vehicles soon cease to run anywhere at all except off the track and into the shag pile, which is forbidden by the manufacturers. If you are energetic enough to return these little speedsters to their manufacturer, the comment will be: 'Aah, somebody has been running these on CARPET'.

So the cars and their tracks are packed away and laid to rest in the boxes in which they were born.

None of the lids ever fit back on.

Our cemetery upstairs is also full of dead dolls, animals which need combing, ugly plastic objects which turn into other ugly plastic objects, board games based on television shows which have passed from prime, hula hoops, go-go balls that went, casks of boring crayons which don't stain, and the gifts with the shortest life span of all . . . educational toys.

Has anyone ever seen a child actually counting the coloured beads on a counting frame?

This year we're not buying any toys at all. Serenity is getting her own laundry basket. She loves dropping her clothes into the wash — it saves her folding them up. Rash is getting a multi-box of batteries. Turbulence is old enough for his first lawn mower and a year's supply of petrol.

And when he's finished using it, we're going to let him keep it in the garage . . . right next to the exercise bike the Good Husband gave ME for Christmas last year.

May it rest in peace.

Part 3

STILL Practising

Once they get into primary school your children's doubts about you are confirmed. But they're resourceful at this age and their energy has not yet been diluted with cynicism. They are willing to try parental retraining.

You may persuade yourself that you are still practising; in the limited amount of time left in the child raising game, there may still be an opportunity to improve your technique. But it's unlikely.

THE BURDEN OF Beaching

Often as I lie awake on sticky summer nights, listening to the mosquitoes running relays between my husband's ear and mine and searching for sleep, I dream about the beach days of my youth.

Way back then, when I was often tanned and sometimes trim, and when I still believed I would grow taller, my sisters and I would grab our towels, race from our holiday flat down to the beach and plunge into the sweet, sharp chill of the sea. I remember sand in the teeth and currents pulling us to certain death, while the life-savers looked on, hard-bodied, brown and languid in their unreachable towers.

I remember how we flung ourselves onto the hot sand and baked our bodies brown, without worrying about skin cancer, pooh in the water or what to feed a family of five when we got home. The heaviest piece of equipment we carried with us was a comb.

To many people, a day at the beach is only a hazy memory. They admit they used to go, but they speak in tones of wistful incredulity, in the same way as they might murmur: 'I used to set my hair in rollers' or: 'I used to wear stockings and stiletto heels when I went shopping'.

It's the sun that has ruined the beach for everyone. Not content to simply roll around heaven all day, that yucky old sun is burning our beach pleasures to oblivion. Then there's the pollution; it's hard to find a wave clean enough to cool off under. As for the life-savers — most of them are white-skinned and weedy, dressed from head to toe in sun-screen and protective clothing — and young enough to be our nephews. Only the very oldest life-savers are still as hard and brown as tree bark . . . but they emerge from the surf club rarely, and generally only in the shelter of a four wheel drive.

How do I know these things? Because there is one large section of the population which continues to go to the beach, despite all odds, to survive the summer school holidays. These people are called parents and we are among them.

Let's face it. The beach is free, it keeps the kids contented and it lasts longer than a movie.

Actually, our family's beach holidays have always been dominated by a single major and all-consuming issue. It's not pollution; it's not cancer; it's not the fact that even on vacation, I still have to cook something resembling dinner, each night. It's equipment.

When the Good Husband and I set out for the beach with Turbulence, Serenity and Rash in tow, every one of us carries part of the beach burden. Nothing is left to chance. But the hearts as well as the arms, are full. Any load relief offered by parents to one child, without an equaliser soon afterwards, is stored in smarting memories.

Armed against the sun, the sea, thirst, hunger, discomfort, boredom and dangers of the deep, we make our slow and cumbersome way from our holiday box to the flagged area of the beach.

The father, in his role as our fearless leader, always takes the beach umbrella. This he carries like a mediaeval lance, under one arm, ready for any unexpected enemy attack from the front, but making it necessary for his troops to walk a safe distance in the rear. Over his other shoulder he carries a gigantic plastic zip bag into which the colour-coordinated Christmas beach towels have been packed. Clasped in his hand are two fold-up beach chairs for all of us to fight over. Around his neck he carries his camera, ready to immortalise forever another year of seaside sulking.

Turbulence comes next, with his most prized possession, a lurid, ridiculously expensive (as he says himself, thank goodness Santa brought it) boogy board, strapped to his back in its special cover. Over one arm he carries the beach rug and with the other hand he half pulls, half carries an inflatable rubber boat, which he purchased himself. Beware the insensitive adult who suggests he might not need both boat and board. Did he not mow lawns for ten hot Sundays to pay for that boat? Where's the justice in denying him his rights to his own assets? All right then, the insensitive adults simply insist that he carries his own assets without complaint. He does.

As a special favour to Turb, Rash follows with three assorted sized buckets containing a variety of spades. It is beneath Turb's dignity to show any connection with these items, even though Rash has never played with them in his life and it is indeed Turb who needs the buckets to keep his hands free of sand and to wash down both his board and his boat. The spades will be used by all the children eventually, to dig a deep deep hole into which they will all fit. They do it every year, usually on the last day, but the spades must be brought along every time, just in case.

Rash also carries his own miniature boogy board under his arm. Unlike Turb's, which matches his swimmers and is clean and gleaming, Rash's board shows signs of human habitation, like teeth marks, texta patterns and a chunk missing from the side, where he decided to see what would happen if he rode his bike over it.

Gasping with exhaustion, her eyes glazed with the agony of having to exert herself, Serenity has the privilege of carrying Big Bertha. Bertha is an overgrown, overblown plastic tyre, with handles, in which all three children ride over the ocean waves for at most five minutes every day while their father takes their photograph. For the rest of the time Bertha lies shyly beside me on the beach, drawing curious looks from passers-by and keeps her fat girth covered with drying towels.

As the female parent, it is my privilege to bring Mum's Basket. About the only thing that is not in it is a comb. Yet the equipment situation has improved since the children were babies.

In those days we took two umbrellas to guarantee shade, a large folding chair for me to sit in while I was nursing, two bags of clothing, a stroller, and a lot of tip trucks. The children were too small to carry anything and we were often lucky to arrive on the beach before they closed it for the day.

These days I spend my time at the beach huddled under our giant umbrella, swathed in melanoma-proof fabric, packing and sorting the vast array of equipment that has become an essential part of a day at the beach.

There are bottles of sun-screen lotion, sunglasses, board wax, oranges to guard against scurvy, vinegar in case of bluebottles, tissues for the public loos, buckets and spades, tip trucks for Rash to run over our toes, headrests, an array of hats and caps, drinking water, towels, straws, match boxes, small dolls to live in Serenity's castles, always assuming Rash has not drowned them first, and books for . . . well, just in case.

When I've finished with my basket I just sit there, under my big hat, keeping watch along with all the other conscientious mothers on the beach . . .

. . . Hoping for a glimpse, just a glimpse, of a very old life-saver.

HAVING A CRACK AT Cricket

'Morning Mum, morning all,' said Rash as he sauntered** into the kitchen. 'It's a beautiful day down here at the breakfast bar and I'm sure all the family are looking forward to an enjoyable day of play.'

Casually he picked up an orange from the fruit dish and bowled it in slow motion into the bowels of the family room couch.

'Howzat?' boomed his father as he came out to find a clean pair of socks. 'What's the score?'

'Twelve for 120, and I got the captain out for a duck.'

'You don't want a duck, we'd have nowhere to keep it,' I said tersely. 'Eat your toast.'

In February the cricket season goes on. And on. Droning away on the teev, occasionally drowning out the cicadas and always taking priority over anything a flesh and blood mother might want to do or say, cricket never seems to end.

Words cannot express how much I hate cricket.

I remember the sticky, stuffy lounge room of my childhood, and the red roll of the back of my father's neck as he sat all through the Christmas holidays, glued to cricket on the box while sticky flies buzzed unnoticed around his ears and my mother begged him to take us all for 'a little drive to the coast'. I remember my first summer romance being cruelly shattered when the boy I adored didn't hesitate when offered a choice between a day in my arms and a ticket to the SCG. I remember how my former brother-in-law held up a hand to silence me as I ran in with the exciting news — he just had to catch the score before he found out whether he had a baby son or a new daughter.

I've tried to get interested. I've tried to sit on the couch, following the play, watching the players chew and squint and gently scratch themselves while they, too, wait for something to happen. Why, in cricket, does it all take so long?

Finally someone hits the ball. It doesn't go very far. The men don't run very fast. If they get to the other end they do. If they don't, they don't. There's none of the high speed base racing of baseball or the thrilling swoop and thwack of tennis.

And now fate has played the cruellest trick of all. Rash has become a cricketer. The extracurricular kid has finally found a passion which puts all his other passions in the shade and leaves him standing for hours every Saturday in the sun. Wearing a vast hat that makes him look like a mushroom on steroids, clad in white from neck to toe, his small but vital regions protected with a small but vital object which is shaped like an oxygen mask and known as 'Hector', he takes his place in a field of other mushrooms, and stands still for longer than he's ever managed in his life.

If Test cricket is slow, Under Nine cricket is eternal. Rash chews, spits, squints, gently adjusts himself from time to time and occasionally holds up a lot of fingers and shouts something incomprehensible like 'Six!' or 'Gone!'

Sometimes he gets to bowl. Sometimes — not often — Rash's ball hits one of the sticks behind the batsman and all the mushrooms run around on their piece of grass and cheer.

Rash has only batted in one game this season. It took him so long to hobble out to the centre with gigantic white air beds strapped to his little legs that it was lunch time before he got there and the fielding team had to go home.

At home, Rash performs amazing cricketing feats with milk cartons, salad servers, fruit, broom handles, and even pillows, while providing a commentary in the alternating accents of Ritchie Benaud and Tony Greig .

'That's a rawther lawge effort,' he murmurs as I carry in the washing basket. 'It's a great crowd here today at the dinner table,' he observes, smacking a pea with his knife as we sit down to our chops and veg. 'That's a pret-ty smooth delivery, wouldn't you say, Max?' he asks as Serenity pours out his milk. The only time he turns himself off is when he turns the television on — and it sounds just like him.

Sometimes he comes home from his matches downcast and depressed and despite myself, my heart aches for him. 'I'll never play for Australia,' he says with a catch in his throat instead of his hand.

'Nonsense,' says his father — for at least this cricket thing has given them a special bond. 'You bowled a maiden over today.'

I try to look interested. 'Never mind,' I say, 'she probably shouldn't have been on the pitch anyway.'

They both look at me with scorn.

Words cannot describe how much I hate cricket.

FETE Accompli

In an era where coming out with shocking truths is very much in vogue, I have to admit it. I have a phobia about fetes.

There are those among you who will argue that nothing in the school year could be as hard to endure as athletics carnivals, which find you huddled on a windy hillside, with only a padded parka to protect you from the biting gale and the triumphant sound of young competitors screaming for tuckshop money.

Others will point out that sitting all day by a pool, surrounded by stopwatch women with charts, or worse still, spending all day running around a pool, chasing a toddler and dodging stopwatch women with charts, is the least pleasant event of the year.

Some parents deny that they get any enjoyment from sitting in a draughty hall and raking the crammed stage with watering eyes as they search desperately for just a glimpse of a child in the back row of the choir who may or may not be singing *Give Me a Home among the Gum Trees* for the fourth year in succession.

But for me, fetes are not just unpleasant, they arouse in my soul an abnormal mixture of guilt and inadequacy that no ordinary suburban mother should have to endure.

From the afternoon when the first fete note emerges, creased and slimy from the school bag, to the big day, when we pass through the school gate and into that sea of hand-made mediocrity, I have fete phobia.

I feel guilty that I cannot bring myself to volunteer for the fete committee. I can't bear the thought of sitting in an unused classroom, on a chair too small for my bottom, discussing ways of getting an already financially stretched community to spend their pleasure dollars on lace-covered tissue boxes, pre-loved dolls in pastel knitwear and miniature rocking chairs made by fourth class from paddlepop sticks.

I feel guilty that I get confused about what week we are meant to send books and magazines and when they need poppas and chips and which weekend Mr Blames' truck is available to pick up junk from our garage.

Besides, we still use the junk in our garage!

I feel bad that I don't belong to an organisation that is willing to donate 650 pencil sharpeners for the show bags and I feel worse that the Good Husband does not work in the sort of place that will provide a computer for the raffle prize or even, perhaps, a chook for the chocolate wheel.

The guilt induced by fete phobia is supplemented by intense feelings of inadequacy. Nobody buys my raffle tickets. I can't roll money. My cakes all sink and the plants I've potted fall down and die. The toffee for the lolly stall cannot be removed from the pan even with an electric drill.

I feel guilty that I can't bake or knit or crochet or bottle preserves. That coat hangers in tulle petticoats don't turn me on, that balding soft toys don't strike me as a bargain, that there is nothing I want less in life than a tin of talc and a doily in a cellophane bag, that I can't understand why any household would need more than one tea cosy.

New South Wales had fifty dry days in a row this year. The Treestump South fete was held on the fifty-first day. Guilt-ridden, feeling that somehow the rain was my fault, I volunteered to work wherever I was needed.

In the craft room they stood me beside a table covered with blue and apricot baby matinée jackets and wastepaper baskets dressed in Laura Ashley. (My own daughter has never been as well dressed as those bins.) A little customer thrust a pipe cleaner twisted into a spiral towards me. 'Five cents,' I said. Myra Brisk, the Craft Manager, whipped around.

'Those are ninety cents each,' she snapped. 'There's a magnet inside.'

I was so busy wondering what one did with a magnet in a pipe cleaner that I mucked up the change. Not for the first time.

'Does six dollars and ten cents sound right to you?' I asked a neat lady who was buying Christmas hand towels and a man made of lids. 'That's exactly why I made ten cakes instead of going on a stall,' she said crossly. 'You tell ME the price. It's YOUR job.'

I was still wondering what one did with a man made of lids when they sent me to the sweets stall.

I sold five bags of rocky road, six jars of marshmallows and ten packets of coconut ice. Then I put my purse away and started serving other people.

There were sums to do and stickies to sort, and all the time I had to dodge around boxes and boxes of Lifesavers, which somebody's father donates every year, but nobody wants to buy until everything else runs out.

When they realised I couldn't cope with the intricacies of lolly arithmetic they sent me out to the drinks stall, which stood in the quadrangle in pouring rain. 'Cool off with a coke!' I yelled. Nobody came near me.

Towards the end of the day I was directed to the face painting room, where I relieved a tall woman on a short chair who almost wept with relief when I arrived. I took over her job of prising money from the sticky fists of very small children; I also had to take their fingers out of the paint pots and keep them in a queue at a safe distance from the heavy-breathing artists who had been painting for four hours. The atmosphere in the damp and stuffy classroom was tense. Riots were imminent.

'Sit down and tell me what you want to be,' I said. They all sat very close. They had been eating an amazing variety of food, most of which was still visible on their teeth and detectable on their breath.

'I want to be a panda,' said one.

'Like this boy?' I asked, as a client with a black and white striped face slid off his stool. He burst into tears.

'I'm Batman!' he said. 'You didn't know.'

Next year I'll know better. I'll be reverting to my usual therapy. On fete day after delivering my children and six months' savings to the school, I will take my cakes to the cake stall, give the ladies there a quick look and buy them back again before anyone notices that they are three-quarters icing. Then I'll accompany my cakes back to my car to wait until the fete is over.

Getting into the back seat with a couple of chocolate cakes won't cure fete phobia, but in the absence of counselling, it eases the pain.

THE SILENT Treatment

'Hi Rash,' I said cheerfully, in my maternal, 'I ought to be congratulated' voice. 'You must have heard me thinking about a great big ice cream, just for you.'

It was a line straight out of the 'Brady Bunch', the warm and welcoming mother greeting the tough little kid as he slammed home from school.

But Rash's eyebrows met in a heavy black V and his bottom lip protruded, pink and pugnacious, above his scornful chin.

'Forget it,' he hissed, stomping past me and out into the yard, where he flung himself down on the browning grass and stared disconsolately at the sky.

There has been a new pattern woven into the rich tapestry of life at No. 1 Frustration Close. Ladies and Gentlemen, we have a sulker!

When I was a tiny girl my mother told me frequently how people who sulked only hurt themselves, never others. It didn't take me long to realise that this was one of the Great White Lies which adults tell to children, along with the one about dentists not hurting and school being fun.

Of course sulking hurts other people. It makes siblings frustrated. It makes parents feel amused, then angry and then as guilty as hell. It drives whole families mad.

The only one to emerge unscathed is the sulker. Wallowing in a warm, self-righteous sea of resentment, he simply removes himself from all hurt and pain. Protected from normal human feelings by withdrawing into petulant silence, he becomes a spectator who watches with detachment as the rest of the family try pleasantness and fail, try ignoring him and fail, try verbal abuse and fail . . . and finally crack, break and begin to tear out each other's throats. Hooray! Sulker 10, Family Nil.

Of course Turbulence never sulked. Sulking requires a certain amount of independence and determination. It also frequently involves a break from normal routines. While sulking and worrying may appear to be related emotions, Turbulence's high anxiety finds its outlet only in communication. When he was younger this took the form of floods of tears. Now he is older, there are floods of conversation. Tears and talk have no part in a sulker's life.

Serenity would quite like to sulk and has tried it on occasions. But while a successful sulker has to be able to keep silent, scorning the company of others, this behaviour is not effective unless it is seen to be abnormal. A girl who rarely speaks unless she has something to say, and spends long hours locked in her room with texta pens, cotton reels and toilet roll cylinders, is not likely to be an effective sulker. Serenity gave up sulking very quickly, simply because nobody noticed.

With the same determination and energy he used to learn how to bowl a cruel curve and hit a boundary, Rash has taken sulking and made it into a highly honed skill. He is very very good. Even the most delectable cakes, the most mouthwatering ice blocks, the fizziest drinks, will not inveigle him into joining the family at snack time. The funniest shows, the most hilarious accounts of Turb's and Serenity's adventures with their friends and victories over their teachers, cannot draw forth a smile from those grim and angry lips. The sternest reprimand, the richest sarcasm, cannot bring softening, sulk-melting tears to those hard eyes.

Rash understands that well-behaved sulkers stop behaving well, while badly behaved sulkers frighten the life out of everyone by silently and resentfully doing what they are told.

So during a sulk, Rash, normally forgetful and naughty, does everything that's required of him and does it well.

Why, you may well ask, would we want to stop him sulking at all?

Because he is smarter than he looks.

Instead of staying in his room he sulks in public places, lying on the lawn in front of the kitchen window as I peel the vegetables, hunching miserably on the concrete driveway as I pull out weeds, ensuring that his hair shirt scratches our hearts for hours on end.

Only when he has reduced the entire family to abject misery will he relent and tell us what we've all done wrong — that we've hurt his feelings. In a variety of ways.

We sigh. We are not used to Rash having feelings, but we don't say that. Instead, we apologise. Five minutes later, to our relief, he's happy and loud and naughty again.

'You should have told us about your problem straight away,' I say reprovingly. 'Sulking doesn't do any good. When you sulk you only hurt yourself.'

But I cannot meet his eyes as I speak and behind my back my fingers are very tightly crossed.

CAMPING OUT Is In

'If we're going to do this at all,' said the Good Husband, his beard swelling with enthusiasm, 'we're going to do it RIGHT.'

I saw the shiver of excitement run down Rash's small spine. I felt the shiver of dread run down mine. I saw Turbulence close his eyes tightly so that his father would not see the anxiety reflected there. Serenity laughed.

Spring has injected new vigour into my work weary husband. It's brought out the adventurer in him. It's given him energy, ambition, courage! Or maybe he's just worried about going grey.

'Madness!' roared Rash and I had to agree.

Because The Men have decided to go camping.

All over suburbia, The Men are starting to sit up and take stock. It's not just the warm weather. It's the magazines and newspaper articles and books which are telling men to get back in control of their lives. To throw off the shackles that the industrial revolution has tied to their ankles, to burn their ties, dirty their white collars, get back to basics, muddy their hands, open their eyes . . . and most of all, be fathers to their sons.

The GH had discovered the men's movement so he was taking his sons and moving out.

The main challenge, of course, was getting equipped. It's always the same with us. We never have what we need for an adventure. Our suitcases are too big, our plastic shopping bags are too small. Every other family we know seems so much better prepared than we ever are. They have picnic baskets with special nooks and crannies for everything you need to eat away from home. They have table and chair sets that you can fold up and keep in your glove box. They have specially fitted bags with compartments for shoes and deodorants. They have eskies big enough to live in. They have tents.

'You can't go camping without a tent,' said Turbulence and his father's face fell. Getting back to nature was one thing, inhaling dew was another. 'We'll have to buy one,' said Rash.

Now here we struck a second obstacle. Being a father to his sons was one thing, spending a lot of money on them was another. Especially when the initial adventure would keep them out for only one night. Besides, the acquisition of material possessions was just one of the sad symptoms of modern manhood that he was hoping to thrust aside.

Luckily the GH's best mate, Sean, had a tent he was willing to lend. He threw in a camping stove and a lantern as well.

'There are no insect screens with the tent,' said Turbulence anxiously after a thorough inspection of the borrowed goods. 'And the ground sheet has holes in it.' He went off to get some insect repellant and a large piece of carpet which had covered his bedroom floor before our renovations. Turb cannot bear to throw any part of his childhood away.

The GH went to the shops and came home with three huge air mattresses and a water bottle. There was some consternation when we blew up the mattresses with the vacuum cleaner and discovered that only one of them would fit inside Sean's tent.

'We could sleep in a row with our chests and heads all on the same mattress and our legs dangling off,' said Rash. The GH looked doubtful. Turbulence, his imagination vivid with the prospect of scorpions and other wildlife nibbling his toes, looked more so.

The water bottle filled up the boot of the car. 'Most camp sites have taps,' I said. 'We're taking our own,' said the GH firmly. 'We're getting back to basics. We're not going to rely on FACILITIES.' He spat out the word scornfully.

The Men were so busy trying to fit the equipment into the car they overlooked a few details. Like food. Serenity and I packed bread, margarine, milk, eggs, tea, sugar, chops, sausages and fruit into the esky. We tossed in a salad.

While The Men wrestled with tomahawks, fishing rods and tent poles, Serenity and I filled two bags with warm clothing, pillows, knives, forks, plates, cups, bowls, toothbrushes and deodorant.

'This is ridiculous,' said Mr Storm, when he saw what The Men needed for a night in the open. 'This won't all fit in the car. We'll have to go on foot.'

'And CARRY it?' asked Serenity. Physical effort of any kind shocks Serenity, even when it's not going to be her own.

Armed with knives, walkmen, sleeping bags and barbecue tools, they set off. We waved, but The Men didn't look back.

About eight p.m. Serenity and I were interrupted during our favourite television program by scratching at the back door.

'We're cold,' said Turbulence.

So I sent Serenity out into the back yard with an extra quilt and a hot-water bottle for each of them.

Women. What would The Men do without them?

TOPIC Trauma

Most of the time and especially in the mornings, when I gently usher my children out the door, I give thanks for the existence and dedication of school teachers with all my heart.

But teachers are only human and inevitably, from time to time, they can't resist coming up with ghastly schemes, as cruel as they are creative, to get back at the mothers and fathers who have saddled them with their unspeakable offspring for six hours a day, five days a week.

Incredibly, they have now invented a form of parent torture even more agonising than school projects. It's called the Topic Talk.

Preparation for a Topic Talk is so absolutely time-consuming and mind-bogglingly boring that comparing it with school projects is like comparing cleaning out the linen cupboard with washing every curtain in the house — and ironing them as well.

Of course, there is a connection. A project involves finding out a lot of information about something nobody is interested in, and putting it on cardboard, together with pictures, samples and fancy lettering which usually smudges before the due date. (Most of the samples, especially if they are bits of unwashed merino or puny wheat seeds, have fallen off their glue base by then as well.)

A Topic Talk involves collecting a lot of information about something nobody is interested in and writing it out on small cards or pieces of paper which never again appear in the same order as the notes were written.

A Topic Talk also involves the collection of pictures and samples, but because these must be held up in front of the class, they have to be large, eye-catching and original. Cutting off a small lump from the lining of your ugh boot will no longer do as a sample of unwashed merino. For Topic Talks, the audience have to be able to FEEL the GREASE. What's needed are large mats or small sheep, whole husks of wheat, chunks of coal, sheets of steel, life-sized posters of Sir Donald Bradman, enormous dolls dressed as Caroline Chisholm and preferably live mammals breast-feeding their young.

On completion of a school project, the book or cardboard has simply to be handed over to the gloating teacher, by the red-eyed child and its grey-complexioned, sleep-starved mother. The Topic Talk, on the other hand, has to be presented to the whole class — and to practise that, the child needs a captive audience.

Available audiences are not easy to find in your average suburban home. There's something about the nature of a Topic Talk in rehearsal that leaves the stalls empty. There's usually only one person willing to watch — again and again and again.

Over and over you hear the words, as you slump on the kitchen stool, clutching the stopwatch, willing the seconds to fly by. You try to thwart the boredom by correcting, suggesting, offering advice. Nothing you say is of any use. What would you know, Mum? That's NOT what the teacher said to do. Yet once through is never enough. You have to hear it one more time. And again. And just once more. And this time, Mum, they promise, they'll get it right.

A panel of classroom judges will mark the Topic Talk. They have been told to award points for information, presentation, props and eye contact.

Eye contact! You've been demanding it unsuccessfully for years while you've gone on about truth and obedience and doing unto others. Suddenly they can stare unblinking into your wavering gaze for hours on end as they spout the distinctive habits of Australian mammals, list the rivers of New

South Wales in geographical order or jabber about Japanese cultural customs.

At least for a project the teacher has to read all thirty pieces of cardboard! But during a Topic Talk, she sits smirking at her desk, a good novel discreetly tucked behind a heap of textbooks. She's laughing all the way through the reduction of her stress levels.

Mrs Tweed slipped up this term. She made the mistake of letting the students choose their own Topic.

Suffering severe withdrawal symptoms following the end of his cricket season, Thug decided to prepare a Topic Talk on his favourite sport. He began with a history of the game, and followed it with a detailed description of all the Ashes matches for the last twenty-five years. He then demonstrated every bowling style and every batting stroke ever invented since the first thwack of willow.

Apparently he put everyone in the class to sleep except his teacher. He introduced his Topic Talk with the words: 'I know how much Mrs Tweed will want to hear this because she LOVES cricket,' and then maintained rigid eye contact with her throughout.

Okay, so I had suggested the intro and fiddled the stopwatch a little on each of his forty-seven practice runs. Okay, so his talk was eight glorious minutes over time.

Revenge is sweet.

SHARING WHOSE Load?

I've been sitting in the family room for two hours, pretending to watch a show on television where the more anguished the women get, the less their lips shine.

But really I've been watching the washing up.

Out of the corner of my eye I can see the kitchen sink. I can see the fat congealing around the edges of the frying pan and the bits of salmon sticking to the sides of Serenity's lunch box. I can't see the drops of gravy on the bench top, but I know they are there, just as I feel the presence of the ants who are probably holding a meeting right now, to decide if they will invade the sweet stickiness of the plastic mugs first or go straight for the peanut butter slime on the carving knife.

As tired as they are, my heavy limbs throb with the desire to rise, to fill the sink with hot soapy water and dispense with the mess.

But I'm not going to.

We have a new rule at No. 1 Frustration Close. Armed with statistics and a press release from the Office for the Status of Women, we have joined ranks to fight the housework battle. With the blessing of the government, we have decided to Share the Load.

Of course, it's not as simple as it sounds.

Let me welcome into this story the father of the Storm children, my Good Husband, a man bred in romantic Ireland, where boys were born to be men and girls were born to wear aprons.

Don't misunderstand. The GH has never objected to giving a helping hand around the house.

'If you tell me what you want me to do, I'll do it,' he says willingly. And he does. 'Would you wash up?' I say. So he fills the sink with water and whatever dishes happen to be within reach are dunked in the suds and plonked on the draining board. Uneaten goo and gravy leavings are slopped into the suds to make a fine brown broth which he leaves there as a solidifying monument to his worthiness. Finer details such as wiping down surfaces, collecting errant glasses and plates which may not be placed immediately to his left, not to mention cleaning up the sink itself, are chores left for the apron wearers. I asked him to wash up. He washed up.

'Would you put Rash to bed?' I ask. 'Get ready for bed!' he roars from his favourite chair and half an hour later he walks all the way up the hall and turns out Rash's light. Medication, teeth cleaning, room tidying, story reading, clothes folding . . . perhaps a helpful little leprechaun took care of that stuff when the Good Husband was a child.

The GH is not the man Hugh Mackay had in mind when he wrote in his report on *Men and Women*: '. . . they are living through a period of unprecedented reappraisal and redefinition of their respective roles in society . . .' The GH's view is that if he wasn't defining himself at his office for ten long hours a day, there wouldn't be a home for any of us to clean. What's to reappraise?

But I am definitely the person Michael Bittman must have had in mind when he wrote in his book *Juggling Time* that women do seventy per cent of the unpaid work in the house.

So we all discussed Sharing the Load. Or more accurately, Sharing My Load.

The children already make their beds, set the table and empty the dishwasher. Turbulence pointed out that despite an overload of homework, he keeps his room immaculately neat (he files his socks) and has recently begun manicuring the lawn for us. (He's asked us very nicely to remove our shoes before walking on the grass.)

Serenity said if she had to do anything else in the morning she would have to give up either piano practice or going to the toilet. It seemed to be an impossible choice.

Rash offered to sharpen my kitchen knives, make fires in the winter or possibly whack all the dead branches from my shrubs but he was pretty cool on the alternative suggestion that he clean his own shoes.

In the end it was decided that every night each member of the family would take a turn at washing up the things that don't go in the dishwasher.

Tonight Turbulence has a maths assignment. Serenity has to finish her collage of bits of Michael Jackson (when I did art at school we learned to draw trees!) before she washes her hair. Rash is just back from soccer training and is now locked in the bathroom, castrating *Unchained Melody* on his trumpet.

The Good Husband has been home to eat his required daily intake of potatoes and has now gone to cancel them out on the squash court.

'The general issue of double load has already attracted international interest . . .' says my press release.

So with international interest on my side, and in the full knowledge that tonight is not MY night to wash up, I'm going to sit here with my unshined lips pressed tightly together and I am NOT going to do the dishes.

Yet.

BATTLE Cries

He smelled the way he always does at the end of a school day, of stickiness and sweat, with an aroma of banana peel and playground dust hanging in the air around him.

But he didn't look the same. His eye was squeezed shut in a pillow of purple skin, a pink cut oozed on his cheek and his shirt was torn and missing the buttons.

Believe it or not, it was Rash's first fight.

Although he talks tough and he is always armed to the teeth, Rash has a healthy respect for anything bigger and stronger than he is. He stalks carefully through life, always alert to signs of danger.

Apart from thrashing a number of my prime shrubs and occasionally menacing the neighbourhood cats, Rash has always avoided actual physical violence. He has exchanged a thousand cuts and thrusts and kicks and blows but all of these have been mimed, mostly in slow motion. Flesh has rarely, if ever, met flesh. Until now.

'These guys threw their ball on to my handball court,' said Rash. 'I caught it with one hand . . . without even looking . . . and chucked it over the fence. So they came and got me.'

He squinted his eyes and we both pretended we couldn't see the tear that threatened to run down one grimy cheek. 'I was concentrating on my serve,' he said. 'If I'd been ready for them they wouldn't have stood a chance.'

What a dilemma it is for mothers to see their small sons' skin, that exquisite tissue they have stroked and washed and nourished so carefully, opened up and bloodied by bullies in the school playground. Women are worried about explicit cartoons, we deplore violence, we want an end to the futility of war. Yet when our sons come home with boot bruises on their faces, we have to crush an overwhelming urge to rush to the school and punch certain skulls into pulp.

This time experience helped me. I didn't make a fuss. I didn't rave or rant or ring the school. I made an icy compress for him to hold against his wound and we sat still together and watched 'The Simpsons'.

When our first child, Turbulence, was a little boy, I was a terrier Mum. I earned a reputation for rushing in to snap at the heels of the horrible little boys who hurt him, yapping at the headmaster about safety in the playground, barking at the parents who told me boys would be boys.

I performed sentry duty along the school fence, making sure no eight-year-old ruffians were denting my son.

Turb was always getting into fights. Gentle, anxious, law-abiding Turbulence was so rigidly fixed on rules that he simply couldn't cope with children who broke them. It took him years to learn that it's dangerous to tell boys three times your size that it's not their turn on the handball court, that their noise is disturbing the kindy kids, that they're supposed to wait for the crossing lady before walking out on to the road.

They pushed him. They shoved him. They tore his shirt and tripped him over. He went down tear-stained, fanatical and unrepentant, still explaining what they were doing wrong, still pointing out where they shouldn't be, still chastising them even as they sat on his head to nullify his nagging.

They never broke him. Most of them went on to high school with their nerves shot, the sound of Turb's voice still ringing in their ears.

But they broke me. I have turned into a mother who would rather not get involved. I have become a pussycat who looks the other way.

So when we were both calm, I hugged Rash and bathed his wounds and we talked about the stupidity of people who resort to violence. We discussed conflict resolution and the benefits of balanced discussion. We talked about his brilliant serve.

I wrote no notes, I issued no threats. Resolutely I stayed away from the phone.

The Good Husband, a man of peace despite being born in the battle zone of Belfast, looked troubled when I told him the bad news about Rash. The GH is not a terrier. He's a big, gentle Labrador. He wouldn't kill an ant unless it was necessary to put it out of its misery.

His face grew longer and longer until it threatened to disappear into his beard. But I pointed out the bright side of what had happened. 'Rash has spent most of his life getting ready for a fight,' I said. 'I feel sure this has taught him how senseless and cruel fighting really is.'

'Why don't you go in and kiss him goodnight, and remind him that violence never solves anything?'

The GH tip-toed gently into Rash's bedroom and sat on his bed.

'You were probably practising your serve,' I heard him say.

'I was,' whimpered Rash.

'You probably weren't ready for them.'

'I wasn't,' breathed Rash.

'Next time you'll be ready for them!'

'Yeah!' yelled Rash.

'Next time, son,' growled the GH, sounding very much like an angry Alsatian, 'they won't stand a chance!'

When he came back into the kitchen the Good Husband glared rebelliously into my accusing eyes. He didn't say a word, but he lifted his big foot and stamped VERY HARD on a passing ant.

That's life.

WANTED URGENTLY: FIFTEEN MORE MORNING Minutes

Now that third term is under way, I suppose I may as well admit that none of the January resolutions have worked. Especially the one about getting up fifteen minutes earlier in the morning.

Where does it go, that precious, desperately necessary quarter hour before nine o'clock?

Where can I find time in the morning to colour in my face, so that I will look like Everyone Else's Mother? Why won't Turbulence talk about his traumas at sunset instead of sunrise? Why don't my children stroll into the school playground at eight forty-five a.m., instead of falling through the gate with socks askew and back packs gaping, just in time for the final bell?

Can it really be traced right back to my reluctance to push away my determined doona in order to begin another day of running fifteen minutes late for everything?

Yet how can I be blamed for the fact that when I finally arrive in the kitchen, showered, dressed and determinedly smiling, I find Turbulence waiting, hollow-eyed and dry-throated, to discuss with me his first Deep and Serious Problem of the day?

My words of encouragement and wisdom invariably send him straight to the toilet, which is my signal to wake up Rash, a complicated routine which involves kissing him quickly on his pillow-warm cheek and then leaping back very quickly to escape the flailing fists with which he invariably greets a new and potentially violent day.

Forced to use the parental toilet, because Turb will be on the other one for hours, Rash rarely returns. He can be heard racing around various parts of the house which do not contain his school uniform, repairing his sword, collecting rope for the prisoners, and finding rubber bands, pencil leads, dead insects and other equipment which has to be checked before such trivial matters as putting on his clothes and eating his breakfast.

Meanwhile I am in the kitchen wrestling with the lunch combinations. Turbulence has real cheese and tuna. Rash has pretend cheese and peanut butter. Anything firmer takes too long to eat. There's nothing like too much chewing to undermine you in the eyes of your troops.

Serenity has gone off cheese and pineapple as it makes the bread soggy. For health reasons, I feel I should veto her order of plastic cheese and tomato sauce, although it's a temptingly easy alternative and it might help me save fifteen minutes.

I have tried following my friend Moana's advice by cutting a week's supply of sandwiches and freezing them. It doesn't work. You can guarantee that before the gladwrap has even got a grip on itself, the kids will have gone right off whatever ingredients are inside.

Turbulence kisses me goodbye. His bag is neatly packed, his bed is made just the way he likes it, his eyes are red. With his hair polished and his shoes shining, he strides off to the bus stop, taking his Serious Problem, my aching heart and an extra handkerchief with him.

Rash is located and camouflaged; to any passing stranger he now resembles a normal schoolboy. The same passing stranger would not have time to hang about and watch me visibly aging as I wait for Serenity to finish her breakfast.

She can make a finger of toast and jam last 15 minutes. Before I dispensed with morning protein she held the world record of one hour, forty-five minutes to consume a boiled egg.

Serenity is not a breakfast person.

I clear off the bench, bellow orders (the resolution never to raise my voice went down the tube on January 2nd), sign permission slips, dole out bus money and check homework. Homework?

Serenity guarantees a drop in my self-esteem by asking me to 'quickly check' her maths problems. This reminds Rash that today he has to take in at least six pictures of people doing Jobs which Help Others.

He says six photos of me won't be acceptable.

The hands of the clock move inexorably on. I scrabble through magazines with my left hand and apply mascara with my right. The current affairs man has taken over on the radio which means it's time to leave. Meanwhile two definitions of eternity are taking place in the Storm house: Serenity making her bed and Rash cleaning his teeth . . . the only child in Sydney who can do this without ever actually placing the brush inside his mouth. He makes up for it by using a tremendous amount of toothpaste.

A miracle. We are actually at the door. Serenity has forgotten her library book, her bus money and her homework. Rash is having a good day; he has only forgotten his 'news'. He has been saving half a golf ball which he found rotting in the reserve. He dumps his schoolbag in the driveway and races back into the house.

If we had left fifteen minutes ago we would have been on time.

I guess it's about as futile as saying if I'd looked behind me as I backed the car out I wouldn't have run over Rash's school bag.

It's days like these when I wished I'd talked him out of cheese and peanut butter.

A YOUNG MAN'S Fancy ...

Romance is blossoming at No. 1 Frustration Close. Our toes might be frozen, our gardens are bare, but looking at the dazed and distracted expression on a certain little face, it might as well be spring.

No, it's not Turbulence. Turbulence is too wrapped up in himself to dream about the opposite sex. I once asked him how many girls were in his class and he said one, he thought, whereas there turned out to be twenty-three!

Before he left for his first school dance we told Turb that he should stop worrying about himself long enough to compliment his dancing partner, who would also be nervous. He came home feeling very pleased with himself. 'I did what you told me, Mum. I said: "You look very nice tonight John".'

He did have a girlfriend when he was ten. His friends all had one. They convinced him he should acquire a friend of the opposite sex as well. So he obliged. Showing a troubling lack of imagination he chose the same girl to 'go with' as all his mates. She was Legsy Swift, the fastest runner in Year Four.

Legsy could out run anybody under twelve, girls and boys alike. She used to throw Turb and his friends an occasional friendly wave as she thundered past them on the running track. Once a clod of mud kicked up by Legsy's spikes hit Turb on the cheek. It was a sign of his devotion that he didn't cry. But Legsy moved away and Turb went back to colour coding his cassette collection.

And it isn't Serenity. If our pleasant, serene, easy-going daughter has ever been in love, nobody has noticed. I imagine that if Serenity wanted a boyfriend, she would probably make one out of polystyrene and cardboard cylinders. He would be quiet and manageable, just like her. Bits of him would probably end up lying around the house but that would make him compatible with Serenity as well.

It's Rash who is in love. He went to the school disco dance and it seems he danced with Didja Reilly all night long. Didja has a reputation! She is the only girl in the school whose video game scores are consistently higher than those of Rash and his friends.

If you think Rash in love is pretty hard for us to take, spare a thought for his disciple and adoring friend, Mat. Mat is a beautiful boy, soft-eyed, sensitive and intelligent, and so similar to my first-born, Turbulence, that I occasionally wonder whether the stork read his street directory wrongly the week he delivered him.

Like Turb's, Mat's feelings are fragile and frequently exposed to the world. While they always accepted him exactly as he was, Turb's friends never had the time nor the inclination to assist his self-esteem; neither do Mat's. Rash has been walking on Mat's feelings for years, which often causes me a great deal of distress — more distress, in fact, than it appears to cause Mat himself, who hangs in there for better or worse, providing forgotten homework sheets, knowing where Rash last left his sneakers and choosing Rash for his partner for every Responsible Errand on which the teachers send him.

There is no doubt in my mind that Turbulence and Mat will grow up to be sensitive new age men. But I've always been concerned at the absence of Rash's sensitivities, which seem to be limited to his continually itchy skin. Would love, I wondered, save him? At least in the past, Mat's only opposition for Rash's affection had come from other boys. But in the car, driving them to cricket practice, I was subjected to a conversation I wasn't meant to hear.

'I saw you dancing with Didja Reilly,' I heard Mat say.

'Didja?' said Rash, glancing carelessly out of the window.

'It's boring dancing with one girl all the time, isn't it?' said Mat.

'Really?' asked Rash coolly.

'Do you remember kindergarten?' asked Mat after a short silence.

'Barely,' said Rash, with the disdain of a man who received his discharge papers more than two years ago.

'But do you remember Frillene?'

'No.'

'She was the girl whose breath smelled like stale bread.'

'Oh, HER.'

'Yep. When we had dancing lessons in kindergarten they told us to choose our favourite person for a partner. Remember?'

'Yes.'

'And I asked you, of course.'

'Of course.'

'But you were picked. So then I asked Dan and Josh and Pete and Thomas. And they were all taken by the other guys.'

'The cool dudes always get picked first,' murmured Rash.

'I know. So then I had to ask girls — Lisa and Linda and Brooke and Meadow and Sky.'

'The cool girls,' said Rash, still staring out of the window.

'They were all taken,' went on Mat blithely. 'So I had to stand against the wall with the ones who weren't picked. And I got Frillene. And I had to dance with her for a whole year.'

Rash sighed. 'It's better to be cool,' he explained — rather needlessly, I thought. 'Didja Reilly's cool.'

'Rash?' said Mat nervously, after a short, painful pause.

'Hmmm?'

'I'm not cool, am I?'

For one long moment my son's eyes met mine in the rear vision mirror of my car.

With all the maternal force I could muster I shot a jet-propelled stare into the glass and watched it reflect back onto his face. I sent Rash a look of incredible intensity designed to snap him out of his lovesick dream. Wordlessly but with all my motherly mental might, I willed him to be kind to the boy who had been a much better friend than he deserved.

'Of course you're cool, Mat,' my son mumbled at last.

Relief quivered and gulped in the air between the three of us.

'Not as cool as me,' Rash added, ' but cool.'

My heart expanded with happiness. Thank heavens. My little boy had learned to lie.

Love does that to people.

MEN AT Work

The dust caking thickly on our sheet-shrouded furniture looked like newly fallen snow. Dust danced in the air, clung to the curtains and hid in my nasal hair. Over the sound of screaming drills, the phone was ringing. I had no idea where it was.

I walked into the war zone and closed the front door on the sight of our old bathroom and kitchen, lying in jagged slabs on top of my azaleas.

'G'day,' drawled a man on a ladder. 'Been out spending your husband's money again?'

We're renovating.

That's all I need to say as an introduction, really, isn't it? Those of you who have no need to renovate will roll your eyes into the top of your heads in the same way that thin people do when their friends mention diet. And turn the page. Those of you who have been through the nightmare will read on hungrily, desperate for a clue to survival, hoping despite yourselves that the Storm family are faring even worse than you did.

Like most people, the Good Husband and I have been renovating on a moderate scale ever since he removed his tux and I my veil. During the course of our marriage, when we haven't been ferrying our children to sporting and cultural venues, our weekends have been given over to repairing, painting, papering — and nailing bits of our house back on.

These days the time available for turning No. 1 Frustration Close into a dream house is in short supply. Painting the lattice has just taken us five years. It took me six weeks to get to the hardware store for a bath plug.

So when I say we are renovating, I don't mean we are doing it ourselves. This time it's different. This time The Men are here.

First we invited the Professionals. They wore virgin pine aftershave and knew exactly what we wanted. Nothing was a problem. Of course, what we realised after we'd signed was that it wasn't a problem for them because we would never see them again. Instead they sent The Men.

The Men came with their sharp tools and blunt boots. They had narrowed eyes, thin hips, pursed lips and big mobiles. The Men jackhammered our bathroom to oblivion and heaved out our kitchen. They were Men of Action who smashed straight into their work, regardless of noise or mess or the family under their feet. They were Men of Few Words, with vocabularies generally restricted to one disturbing phrase — 'No worries', and one question — 'Any chance of a coffee?'

The Men were now in control of our home and, unavoidably, our lives. The Men shoved aside our possessions, ignored our children, tore up our lawn with their lorries and interrupted our telephone calls. They scorned the existing fixtures. 'Yull wanna get a new wall oven.'

'But there was nothing wrong with the old one.'

'You haven't seen it lately?'

The Men watched me load the machine full of whites and then turned off the water; they waited until I was panting for a coffee before shutting down the electricity. The Men exchanged knowing, lopsided sneers when I said I was working; they listened to me start a telephone interview for a Serious Story before demanding my immediate presence in the shower recess.

'It's important,' they drawled. 'Where d'you want your soap holder?'

'Here,' I said.

'Y'can't have it here.'

'There, then,' I said.

'Y'can't have it there.'

'Well, where do YOU want to put it?' I asked querulously.

'Anywhere you like,' they said, bored. 'Not a problem.'

'I have to get back to the phone,' I muttered. 'Actually, I'm working.'

They exchanged looks through their knowing, narrow eyes. 'Yeah,' they said.

The reaction from our children has been predictable. Turbulence of course, is shattered. Installing a huge built-in wardrobe in his room meant moving his Precious Possessions, many of them dating back to pre-school. Worse, when the wonder robe was completed, he had to re-file his socks. True, he now has enough shelf space to arrange his shoelaces in parallel lines. But with the renovations continuing, he can't get used to using the upstairs shower, and making toast in the TV room. And although he only thaws bread in it, he is horrified at the sight of the microwave in the hall, beside the potted plant.

There was no question of temporarily storing a carton of saucepans under his bed — emotionally he couldn't cope.

Serenity, not surprisingly, hasn't noticed the renovations. Why should she? Living as she does in a room overflowing with clutter, cardboard, crates and confusion, why would she be bothered by the expansion of her natural environment into the other rooms of the house?

Rash loves it all and in his enthusiasm lies my personal salvation from The Men.

Rash has been in on all the action, hovering around the live wires, crunching his feet on the piles of shattered tiles, leaning on precariously piled boxes of glass panels, salvaging smelly bits of pipe, leaning casually against fresh paintwork. He has watched, questioned, fiddled, pulled, poked and pleaded with the Men to let him help. He has crawled where no one was meant to crawl and shrieked with sudden laughter when The Men were just about to drill a delicate hole.

Faced with Rash's unstinting interest, The Men are beginning to crumble.

'Rash home?' they ask casually as they arrive, their fingers twitching slightly on their drill bits. 'Taking Rash out?' they ask, their squinting eyes widening with hope, when they hear the jangle of my car keys.

To The Men I was once a mere woman. Now they have realised that I am Rash's mother — and the only person at the job site with the power to take him away. Slowly, thanks to Rash, the balance of power is being restored.

'No,' I sometimes reply, with a cruel smile. 'He'll be here all afternoon.'

MAN ABOUT THE House

Renovating is a lot like being on a diet or giving birth. Everyone wants to tell you about their own experience. And no way could you be going through the living hell that they did.

My story is a little different. Because after The Men had installed a new kitchen, bathroom and built-in wardrobes at No. 1 Frustration Close, Daryl arrived. Daryl Davis, Builder. And Daryl was NICE.

Thrilled with the fact that our home now had working parts, yet secure in the knowledge that if any of those parts failed to operate he could no longer be held to account, the Good Husband decided we should go further with our renovations. He wanted to add a room. Actually, he referred to it in hallowed tones as The Room and we were given to understand that when it was finished, it would be entirely his; the rest of us would only venture into The Room by invitation.

The only problem with this concept was that not only was The Room to be adjacent to the kitchen, he planned to put the couch, the television and the stereo in there.

You're probably thinking that the rest of the family soon took over Dad's Room, that it became known as the Family Room. You're wrong. In fact, from the day construction began, it became Daryl's Room and I expect it always will be.

Daryl was reliable, respectful and very clean. 'I've had a shower,' he told us earnestly when he came to measure and quote, as if this was a vital prerequisite of his getting the job.

Daryl rearranged his schedule so that he could knock down walls and clean up most of the mess while we were away on holidays. When we returned he did his best to fit the hammering and drilling into the hours when we were most widely awake. Every night before going home he vacuumed not only The Room but most of the rest of the house as well.

He changed our light globes, repaired the gates, helped Rash with his woodwork project, collected the mail and bought nice cakes for our morning tea. When I offered to make him a coffee, tears of gratitude almost filled his eyes.

Daryl was utterly wholesome. When a window frame slipped from his grasp and hit him on the nose, he said: 'Damn. Sorry. Pardon the French,' before rushing out to keep the blood off the new concrete.

Daryl worked long hours. He was invariably around at dinner time, installing light fittings, rollering paint onto the new walls and staining the skirting boards around our feet while we chewed. Daryl wiped up while telling us little stories about other families he had helped through the renovation crisis. Not to mention his work with the poor and underprivileged.

The children rushed home to show Daryl their merit cards and report their spelling scores. He provided a reliable answering service when I was out and kept my life in order. He greeted me at my own door with messages. 'You'll have to pick up Serenity before seven because remember the GH wants to eat before he goes to squash,' he would say.

Daryl's only problem was with doors. A huge sliding glass door for The Room was constantly promised and never delivered. A Room is not A Room when one wall is nailed over with bright blue boards stamped with the words 'Made in Taiwan'.

While we waited, we got Daryl to install a new front door and a new back door. He put them both on backwards. 'Damn,' he said. 'Sorry, pardon the French.'

Six weeks went by and Daryl became angry. Armed with his mobile, he took himself to the furthest corner of the yard ('you don't want to hear this') and rang the manufacturer. 'Daryl Davis, BUILDER!' we heard him roar, in the same way you could imagine other very wholesome people saying: 'John Paul, POPE!' or 'Elizabeth Windsor, QUEEN!' When he came back down the yard his face was red and the scab on his nose stood out like a beetle. 'It's coming tomorrow,' he said.

But it didn't.

The last straw was that when the door finally arrived, the sliding panels were the wrong way around. Daryl spent four hours changing them and then discovered that in fact, the panels had been right in the first place. He had been looking at the door the wrong way around.

'Hell's bells, Daryl,' I said, through gritted teeth. But how could I be cross with him? 'Sorry,' I muttered, 'pardon the French.'

'Don't give it a thought,' said Daryl. 'You'd be surprised at the bad language I hear from people who are renovating their homes. People who are normally very nice.'

He cut me a fresh slice of apple strudel, to show I was forgiven and we ate it together in his lovely new Room.

The Good Husband was the only person in the family who was not infected by Daryl's enthusiasm. Working longer and longer hours in order to pay for his Room, he wasn't keen on having Daryl under his feet when he finally arrived home. The GH saw Daryl simply as a means to an end. That was his mistake.

Now that the Room is complete and a tribute to his devotion, Daryl comes back regularly to see it, to sit in it and I secretly believe, to make sure it's being well looked after. One evening he found the Good Husband in it, sitting on the new couch surrounded by newspapers and happily watching television all on his own. Daryl checked the skirtings, fiddled with the light fittings and ran his hand appreciatively over smoothly planed surfaces, all the time keeping up his friendly line of wholesome patter; finally the GH got up and stomped off to watch the tiny television upstairs.

Daryl sat down with satisfaction on the couch.

A Man and his Room are soon parted, I reflected. But Daryl Davis, Builder, will love that Room long after we finally get the sliding door to open.

HIGH *Hopes*

You assume, because you live in a big city and because your kids can read and speak in sentences and use a knife and fork and occasionally remember their manners, that you've given them a little sophistication.

Of course, parents should NEVER assume.

The Storm family took an aeroplane trip one long weekend and I discovered that when it comes to polish, they could all do with some spit and a very vigorous cloth.

Even before we set off for sunnier climes, there was the problem of getting Turbulence's boogy board on the plane. He had swaddled it in beach towels before sliding it into the protective case which had cost almost as much as a year's insurance for the family car. But he still stepped forward to the stony-faced clerk at the check-in point and asked her if she would take special care of it for him. 'It's a very good quality board,' he told her as she stabbed buttons and ripped out labels with lethally efficient fingers. 'I saved up for the cover myself,' he added, as she finally and reluctantly lifted her gaze to his. 'I don't want to get it dented,' he said anxiously.

She stared at him in disbelief.

'An optimist are you?' she asked.

'No, actually I'm a Christian,' he replied.

On board, Rash, our youngest, kept interrupting the

steward's set safety spiel by putting his hand in the air and calling out questions.

'What if there's a mechanical fault,' he called, 'and my oxygen mask DOESN'T fall down? What then?

'What if the plane just explodes in mid air? Are there parachutes? Will you be showing us how to put on a parachute?'

Inevitably, none of the children liked the airline food.

'What are these little green things?' asked Rash. 'They're too small for lettuce and too big for peas.'

'I can't eat this meat,' said Turb. 'It's bleeding.'

There was nowhere to put Serenity's dinner because she had covered her tray with scissors, glue and cards and was busily making a replica of the aircraft in which we were travelling out of her sick bag.

'Could I go around and ask everyone for their empty juice cups?' Serenity asked me. 'I could make a whole lot of Barbie drum kits. I could use all the toothpicks for sticks. Nobody's using their toothpicks.'

Because the children were actually sitting in front of us we didn't even hear Rash ordering a rum and coke.

The stewardess cleverly distracted him from his request with an invitation to accompany her to see what the pilot was doing.

'Why?' asked Turbulence anxiously. 'Is the plane in trouble?'

'Will he show us how to do a crash landing in case a hijacker shoots him?' asked Rash.

'I'll just go and get you that drink,' said the stewardess.

As we landed and taxied to a halt, a tiny girl uniquely dressed in a white puff-sleeved dress, white socks and black patent leather shoes, slipped out of the seat opposite and smiled at me. 'I'm seven and I'm travelling alone,' she said conversationally. 'I'm a UM. That's an Unaccompanied Minor. My grandmother is meeting me. She has five poodles and a bird.'

She flicked her long blond braid away from her cheek. 'I can understand why your children didn't like the dinners. The food is indecent and you're expected to bolt it down far too quickly on these interstate hops. I didn't eat my main course at all.'

'Perhaps your granny will have some nice supper waiting for you anyway,' I suggested, grappling with my plastic Big W bags as she swung a snappy tartan travel case over her shoulder.

'There's a little French brasserie just around the corner from her apartment,' nodded the girl.

She disappeared into the crowd and I returned my attention to my own children. The boys were trying to stuff a monstrous paper aeroplane into Serenity's cabin bag. They were all using their school backpacks as flight bags. Sword handles and rifle butts protruded from Rash's. Turbulence had packed his with the A–D section of his tape collection, two clothes pegs for hanging out his swimmers after use and a packet of bandaids.

'Wasn't that wonderful?' I asked them. 'Flying through the night sky? And now we'll find our motel and somewhere to get a snack.'

'Mackers!' they all screamed.

Because they don't have a granny who lives in Surfers Paradise with a bistro round the corner, it will be a long time before my children become sophisticated travellers.

It will be even longer before I travel with them. Five poodles and a bird have more chance of getting back on a plane with me than my children do. I have promised myself that next time I am in the air I will be classified as a UM. In case you haven't guessed, that's an Unaccompanied Mother.

A QUESTION OF Finance

One of the hardest things about being a parent is answering children's questions . . . especially when they rarely want to wait around for your thoughtful reply. Most of the queries children put to their parents should be regarded as purely rhetorical.

When they're two or three, our children start shooting us down with that timeless parent leveller — WHY? As their cunning and vocabulary improve, they extend this to WHY NOT? By the time they reach double figures they're asking: IF SHE CAN, WHY CAN'T I? And then of course, when they enter adolescence we get the immortal: WHY SHOULD I?

On the other hand, there are some intelligent and sensitive questions to which most of us feel required to concoct intelligent and sensitive replies. Queries like: What makes thunder? Where do babies come from? Why is reading more important than watching television? How do you count to several? and What colour are you if you are not a Green? all require a thoughtful but brief response. The operative word here is *brief*. Whenever I accept the challenge of replying properly to a question, my children's eyes glaze over and their lips begin to loll long before we have even completed our introductory synopsis.

Then there are the questions which are impossible to answer. For example: 'The news man said the victim was raked. How would you rake somebody?' or: 'Will I cry when I die?' or 'How would you count to infinity?'

In my opinion, the worst question children ask is: 'Why do I have to use my own money?'

Quite simply, life is too short to answer this question correctly. Forget money management, learning the value of the dollar, and the benefits of financial security. Forget about reminding them how much it costs you to keep them in Weet-Bix and Reeboks. Lie. Tell them they have to use their own money because you've lost your purse.

The issue of pocket money has long been one of extreme aggravation in the Storm household. From the first disastrous day when I decided to dole them out a little cash of their own, my children have had no trouble understanding either its value or its management. What they fail to understand is that occasionally they are supposed to spend it.

Actually, that's not quite true. Turbulence, my careful, anxious son, that same son who files his Lego boxes alphabetically and checks weekly to see that his socks are still in parallel lines in his drawer, cannot keep money. In a development so out of line with his character that I sometimes think he might even be normal, the minute Turb's funds reach double figures, they burn the proverbial hole in his carefully selected, triple compartment wallet.

Every time he hears a new recording from his favourite rock group, John Smith and the Right Notes, he brings himself to the verge of bankruptcy by buying it. The same goes for John Smith T-shirts and posters and magazines containing articles on why John Smith got into heavy metal and what the Right Notes eat when they're on tour.

But he never spends his money on anything ordinary. And he certainly doesn't spend it on anyone but himself. Stamps for his letters to the John Smith fan club in America, batteries to play John Smith on his ghetto blaster . . . all these must be funded by the maternal purse. Like bread and milk, stamps, batteries, bus fares and canteen cheesecake are simply the essentials of life, so why should he have to use HIS money?

Serenity, on the other hand, saves her money for months until she is required to spend it on her friends. I am constantly fascinated by the fact that Serenity and her friends spend most of their lives fighting among themselves and breaking each other's hearts, only to fork out the most extravagant amounts of cash to buy each other brand name gifts when anyone has a birthday or anniversary of any kind.

Only Serenity, who has perfected suffering as an art form, can make a mother feel as small as a cashew nut, simply because that same mother refuses to finance the purchase of a massively overpriced Quicksilver T-shirt for a girl who the week before circulated a note saying: 'This week's person to hate is Serenity Storm.'

'It's not for me,' she sobbed. 'Why do I have to use my own money?'

My youngest, Rash, is paid in coin only, owing to his junior years. During those years, he has never been known to spend a cent of his own. He counts his coins, he sorts them, he slavers over them and strokes them but he and his gold are never parted.

Sometimes when we are out he is tempted to spend. As he never has his money with him, he begs a loan. He never pays me back.

He keeps his money in a drawstring bag under his mattress. Once I suggested that, hurled hard enough, this hefty bag of metal would be a more effective weapon than any of his plastic guns or swords, if he was called upon to defend himself or his family.

But looking slightly shocked, he asked: 'Why should I use my own money?'

THE HIGH COST OF Quality

'**Quality time' must be the most frightening phrase in the** parenting vocabulary. 'Running late', 'toilet training', 'starting school' . . . none of these expressions can compare with 'quality time' when it comes to its power to arouse controversy, blame, panic and sheer unadulterated guilt.

Quality time describes those periods of the day when parents are meant to be with their children, sharing deep and meaningful experiences. Actually, I think even shallow and meaningless experiences are acceptable, as long as you are having them together.

The prospect of quality time makes women everywhere shudder. Career mothers and employees (i.e. career mothers on lower pay) feel forced to fit quality time in somewhere between picking up the children from childcare centres, driving them to extracurricular activities, marking their homework, sorting their washing, and cooking their meals. It's never easy, but to forfeit quality time, they are told, is to risk abandoning their children to a lifetime of maladjustment and misery.

Women at home face an even bigger problem. If you're there all the time, how do you differentiate between quality and quantity? Which particular minutes or hours should be earmarked as special time with the kids?

My friend Moana, a career person, cheats. She has convinced her sons, aged four and five, that sorting the washing is a special game for learning their colours. By combining quality time with housework, she kills two birds with one biodegradable cup.

Whether you go out to work or not, the main problem with quality time is that usually when you're ready for it, your children have just started watching their favourite television program, or have disappeared into someone else's yard or are engrossed in an animated conversation with Everyone Else's Mother, whose life with her children is just one long chapter of quality.

When yours are ready to pay you some attention, you're too busy arranging the more mundane details of their lives — like preparing their food, washing their underwear or just leaving for the job that pays for the designer label clothes they wear.

When my children were very small I used to carefully set aside a special hour when I would sit on the floor and play with them. Dutifully we put puzzles together and hammered pegs into boards and built multi-coloured brick towers. Unfortunately, within seconds of the game beginning, I always began to yawn. Over and over again my mouth would contort with boredom, and eventually the children would begin to yawn too. Their concentration would flag, their eyes would droop and pretty soon, long before the allocated hour was up, I would carry them off to bed.

The minute they were out of the way I would stop yawning. Fresh and free, I now had time for a cup of tea and 'Days of our Lives'. Now THAT's quality time!

Regrettably, children have now become aware that quality time is an essential part of their childhood. Rather than taking their free moments with me for granted, the Storm offspring have begun categorising their time.

'Will you give me a game of handball, Mum?' asks Rash. 'We haven't had any quality time this week and you need the practice.'

After half an hour he tells me he's disappointed in my ball skills and goes in search of someone who can return his serve.

'Can we cook together?' asks Serenity. 'Or doesn't it count as quality time if you're sort of working?' In the end Serenity sort of mixes and stirs and slaps dough into the pan and I sort of wash up all her mess and sort of put everything away. We accompany this activity with a long running conversation about why I won't buy her another brand name jumper and how cooking is not just a matter of making a mess and having someone clean up after you. Next time, I decide, we will watch television together. That way we might get to the end of our quality time still on speaking terms.

Turbulence has never been in any doubt about the perfect way to spend quality time. For most of his life he has earmarked the hour before he goes to bed to keep me up to date with the troubles and worries of his life. I am waiting for him to turn into a sullen, sulky and secretive adolescent who refuses to communicate with his mother.

Well, I can dream, can't I?

We should never have let children assume control of quality time. Take my eight-year-old niece, Demanda, for example. (My sister says she wishes somebody would.)

The other night, with her mother curled up on the end of her bed, clapping in time, Demanda was singing every song on her Franciscus Henry tape. It's a very long tape and after the seventeenth or eighteenth number, my sister casually picked up Demanda's library book and began to read. Demanda was furious.

'You're supposed to listen and clap,' she shouted.

'Well, I'm tired of listening and clapping,' whimpered my sister. 'I'm not enjoying myself.'

'This is quality time,' said Demanda. 'You're not supposed to ENJOY it. It's just GOOD for us. So let's DO it and get it OVER.'

And they did.

FAME AT Last!

'I'm going to be the male lead in our class play,' said Rash, rakishly smoothing his palm over the wave in his hair. 'Would one of you help me with my line?'

'It's my turn to run the school assembly,' said Serenity. 'I've been a prefect all year but they forgot me until now.'

I could barely contain my excitement. After years of waiting, fame had finally come. My children were among the chosen ones at last! All I needed to make my world complete was a folding chair with my name on it in the assembly hall!

At Treestump South Primary School, fourth term is dominated by the performing arts, rather than yearly examinations. In fact Rash hasn't mentioned tests at all, unless they had them the day he had to have his bottom X-rayed after accidentally landing on the neighbour's cat.

'Rash's head is going to be so big,' grumbled Turbulence, who has always been too worried about what might go wrong to risk performing on a public stage. 'And Serenity will get called a try-hard.' Turbulence knew what he was talking about. He has been called a try-hard throughout his school career; unlike his sister he has never mastered the art of trying softly.

'I thought you said all the prefects did was count hats and tell other kids to pick up papers,' I said excitedly, as I scanned my wardrobe for an ensemble suited to Mother of the Prefect. 'Should I buy you a new uniform?'

'I only have two more weeks at the school,' said Serenity sensibly. 'Anyway, it's no big deal.'

'Not a big deal,' I expostulated. 'My daughter is going to stand on the stage in front of 600 people and run the entire assembly and it's not a big deal? '

'Mine is,' said Rash. 'I need someone to listen to my line.'

'How can you be the star of the play if you only have one line?' asked Turbulence curiously.

Rash looked scornful. 'I said I'm the MALE lead,' he explained. 'It's *The Lady of the Lamp* and I'm Florence Nightingale's father. I have to say: 'No daughter of mine is going to be a NURSE!' After that Florence does most of the talking.'

'Who is playing Florence?' asked Serenity.

'Mee Yee Tan,' said Rash. 'I think they chose her because we look alike.'

Even Turbulence looked slightly startled. I opened my mouth to say something politically incorrect, then shut it again.

'You know what I mean,' said Rash — but I didn't. 'We've both got black hair,' he added. Then he sighed. 'But you can see the problem.'

I looked quickly at Serenity and Turb. They were nodding seriously.

'Mee Yee's taller than you,' said Serenity.

'Exactly,' said Rash. 'And I'm supposed to be her FATHER.'

We dressed him in long trousers and Serenity's black waistcoat. We added some years by giving him a plastic moustache and powdering his hair white. We cut two sideburns from our old ugh boot — yes, the same one we slice into for sheep and wool projects — and we stuck them to his round and rosy Irish cheeks with sticky tape.

'They'll fall off,' said Turbulence.

Assembly Tuesday finally came. I sat at the back of the hall and swallowed hard as Serenity came forward to the rostrum, her hair shining, her pleats short but sharp as knives.

'Good Morning teachers, boys and girls,' she said clearly. 'I am Serenity Storm, your school prefect. I will now ask the teachers to present their reports.'

She sat down and a number of teachers read reports about test results, sporting competitions, special events and coming attractions. Lines of children stumbled onto the stage to receive merit cards and have their hands shaken by the principal. The deputy gave a lecture about uniforms, manners and vandalism. He introduced a visitor who spoke about bike safety. This all took a very long time. At the end of it, Serenity returned to the microphone. My feet had gone numb and I was so involved in doing a silent little tap dance to bring them back to life that I almost missed her.

'Thankyou for your attention,' she said. 'We will now sing the school song.'

It was over. Serenity had been right about the estimated size of the deal. Still, even though Turbulence had warned me not to clap, I did.

She still hadn't forgiven me by Thursday, when I returned to the school to watch Rash's play.

His line was a triumph. Mee Yee gazed down at him with such filial devotion that you knew immediately Rash was her dad.

My eyes misted over for the second time in two days and a wave of peace and goodwill filled my soul. Fleeting as it was, fame had been bestowed on two out of three of my children. Rash's sideburns had not fallen off. And the owners of the squashed cat had never sent a bill.

That's what makes motherhood worth it!

GOODWILL TO All...

Joseph wore a brown robe and white sneakers and looked relieved when Mary sank to her knees to do something complicated to the baby. Even kneeling she was almost as tall as her husband.

The cows sang lustily beneath their cardboard horns, the donkey hit its head on the microphone and the shepherds looked anxiously for their mothers in the audience.

Down in the hall we parents nodded and clapped and jerked our heads this way and that to avoid blocking the viewfinders of the fathers with video cameras — those men who would have to go home and watch the film to find out if they enjoyed the show.

The men without equipment stood in the side aisles with their arms folded, slightly removed from the mothers and grandparents, wearing expressions of deep concentration.

As if they didn't know what happened next.

We could hear the angels shuffling and giggling off stage. The Angel Gabriel was trying to keep them quiet. Like most men with a lot of women to control, the Angel Gabriel was having a hard time.

And that's just the problem with Christmas, isn't it? The original Angel Gabriel started it all centuries ago when he gave the shepherds THOSE orders. Joy to the World. Peace on Earth. And what was probably the Angel Gabriel's favourite — GOODWILL TO MEN.

For women, who already have their hands full with Joy (baking, decorating, making costumes, shopping, shopping and shopping) and Peace (trying to control tears and tempers of concert-cranky, party-weary, hyped-up kids who've been living for weeks on chips and chocolate and late nights), Goodwill to Men is REALLY hard.

Against considerable odds, women work hard at Joy and Peace. We soothe, we smile, we clap, we praise, we beg, we bribe. 'Santa's spies are listening to you!' we shout joyfully as we race to the laundry tub to soak red food colouring from the Angel Gabriel's robe.

'One more fight and I'm taking all the presents back!' we shriek peaceably as we slump over stacks of Christmas cards.

But Goodwill to Men? How do you show that?

Men themselves don't do a lot of obvious pre-Christmas peacemaking. Nor do they get heavily involved in the joy of stapling antlers, mixing dip, icing fairy cakes, wrapping presents or making streamers. Nor do they shop, until an hour or so before closing time on Christmas Eve.

Don't misunderstand. I have a very Good Husband, a sensitive old age guy. He has his little faults and foibles, like trimming his moustache over my make-up drawer so that my compact and pots look as if they've attracted a sprinkling of image-conscious ants. And stuffing his dirty clothes into heaps at the back of the cupboard. And occasionally forgetting my name. But for most of the year I have no trouble showing him Goodwill.

Until Christmas arrives.

What makes it hard is that Christmas affects his health.

Last year, just before Christmas, he burst through the front door with a face the colour of avocado dip and collapsed on the couch, just as we were in the final stages of looping the tinsel over the Christmas tree.

Seeing his father home early, Rash was so overjoyed he forgot about hanging reindeer by their throats from the lower branches and raced to get his chess set. 'Quality time!' he bellowed above Bing Crosby, but the GH uttered a low moan and crashed his way through bales of tinsel towards the bathroom. Unfortunately, the Christmas tape ran out just in time for the rest of us to be treated to a full-scale stereophonic rendition of the GH bringing up his lunch. And breakfast. And possibly the previous night's dinner as well.

'I hope it's not catching,' said Turbulence anxiously. 'I've got to go to the pool.'

'And I have a rehearsal,' said Serenity.

'You'd better go to bed,' I suggested to their father, in a Goodwillish way, even though my mouth was full of string.

Half an hour later I found him lying limply on top of the bedspread. Of course he had been too ill to remove a pile of ironing before he collapsed.

'A little too much Christmas cheer?' I asked.

'I think I need a bowl of chicken broth,' he moaned feebly. 'I may be dehydrating. Could you get it for me?'

'It's forty-one degrees in the shade outside,' I said, and the Goodwill was thinning fast. 'What about a glass of water?'

'You give soup to sick people and I'm sick,' said the GH, Irish rebel, Gaelic chief, descendant of warrior hordes. 'And could I have a damp cloth for my forehead? If it's not too much trouble?'

When I came back, Rash was lying on our bed, peering into his father's face.

'Dad's moustache goes right up into his nose,' he said. 'Can he come and play cricket with me?'

'I'm DYING here,' croaked the GH, so I helped Rash climb off the ironing and we went downstairs together. 'If he dies,' Rash asked, ' can I have the drill we're giving him for Christmas?'

I drove Turbulence to the swimming pool and Serenity to her nativity rehearsal and returned to clean up the bomb site around the Christmas tree. I bowled two overs to Rash, brought in the washing, cooked the dinner, set the table and left again to collect the big kids. We ate and washed up and I folded the washing and made the Christmas cake. When the children went to bed I wrapped twenty-seven presents. Finally I staggered to bed — but not to sleep. The GH tossed and turned all through the long, sweaty night.

When I peeled open my crusty eyes the next morning, he was glowing above me, freshly showered and wearing a crisp shirt.

'I'm shaky but I have to get in to work,' he said. 'Don't wait for me for dinner. They're having drinks for the department this afternoon. I don't want to let them down.'

I said nothing. I think I even squeezed out a small and only slightly sardonic smile.

Come on, Gabriel. Show me a better will than THAT!

Part 4

YOU REALISE YOU'VE ruined my life?

If the children haven't already convinced you, you now have physical and verbal proof that everything you have made them eat, learn and do has been wrong for them. Their bodies string out or turn lumpy, their teeth go to war, their skin breaks out, their friends often hate them and it's all your fault.

Apart from that, Everyone Else's Parents are still around, financing trips to the movies while you make them use their own money, letting them get up and dress ugly while your obsession with colour coordination, leather school shoes and healthy hair means your child has to go out in public looking like an alien. And of course EEPs leave town most weekends so their kids can have parties at which they do things you don't even want to think about.

You've run out of excuses. You realise you can't win. Ever.

BIRDS, BEES AND Bull Dust

Sex has raised its flushed face again at No. 1 Frustration Close. Families just can't get away from the facts of life. No matter how much you try to impress upon your children the importance of study, no matter how many soccer matches you take them to or how many hours you make them pound the piano, sooner or later it seeps into their curious little minds that something a little more than education, sport and culture is responsible for providing the world with people.

You would think with puberty exploding all over our house that the latest interest in all matters sexual had come from the older children. Not at all. So frightened are both Turbulence and Serenity of demonstrating any sign at all of their bulging biological transition that Turb has converted his skateboard into a barricade (a fairly easy structural operation) and installed an electronic intruder alarm over his door handle (a more complicated measure which is doubling as his science project).

Serenity is wearing two of her big brother's cotton singlets at a time, in a futile effort to push the evidence of her growing femininity back into her chest.

No, it is our youngest, Rash, who came home from cub camp with a newly aroused curiosity about the human reproductive system and all that goes with it.

'Daniel said making a baby is perfectly disgusting,' said Rash with horrible fascination, 'and when his time comes he's going to get his Dad to come over and do it for him'.

With a heavy heart I realised the time had come to tell him about the birds and bees. And to think he'd joined cubs to learn about knots!

Although sex education has now been bravely taken on by schools, the Good Husband and I have retained our masochistic desire to fire off the first salvos ourselves.

Why? Well, for parents like us, who still believe that sex is in some way connected with love, commitment, even (shock, horror) marriage, community sex education has its limitations. The law requires that teachers present children only with the scientific facts. No moral judgements are permitted. This means children from as young as eight get to know every sticky detail about how to make a baby, without being told how much it costs, how much it hurts and how much it matters.

Of course with today's community awareness of all things sexual, when even ice block commercials ooze phallic symbolism and blue denim is designed to pump genes, providing accurate information to children is probably an improvement on the days when anything to do with gender was regarded as a dark and dirty secret.

The nearest I ever came to hearing sex discussed in mixed company at school was during a biology lesson when I was fifteen. The subject was reproduction.

The young male teacher began by explaining the relevant bits and pieces of the human body. Somehow when we reached the point of uniting the bits with the pieces, we were no longer talking about men and women but about cows and bulls. I never did work out where and when the transition from man to beast had taken place but my imagination ran riot.

Determined to do a better job than this, I was ready when our eldest child, Turbulence, asked me where he had come from. I sat him on the couch and told him as gently as I could what was involved in the making of a baby. I tried to keep it technical although I stressed love, commitment and marriage. The more I talked, the more anxious Turb appeared to be. I should have known it would worry him. How could a boy who suffered from nervous tension when his Lego wouldn't stand up straight and who went limp with worry if the school bell was late in ringing, be expected to cope with the uncertainty and unreliability of sexual matters?

After I had struggled to an uncomfortable climax he was silent for a while. Then he looked up at me with large tragic eyes.

'I meant was I born in Sydney or Newcastle?' he explained. But it was too late. He now knew it all. Sex opened a vast new range of topics for him to worry about.

A few days later he told me that he didn't think I had properly covered the topic of contraception. I feel reasonably certain that Turbulence will one day invent the world's first full-body condom.

Serenity, in her calm and casual way, shrugged her shoulders at sex education in the same way that she threw off suggestions that she should make her bed in the mornings or attempt now and then to stagger from the table to the sink with her dinner plate.

'It's okay, Mum,' she said carelessly, when I tried to sit her on the couch. 'I read it all in the encyclopaedia already.'

As she refused to listen to another word from me on the subject I gritted my teeth and took her to a Family Life lecture at the school. She was scornful, declaring the whole night to be a waste of time.

'Well, you have brothers,' I said. 'Some of the girls who don't have brothers may not have understood how girls and boys are different.'

'But they didn't even tell us the main thing,' she said in exasperation. 'They never once mentioned that girls have longer hair.'

Rather than forcing her back to the couch I waited two more years, and then accompanied Serenity to a 'self-esteem course' which the primary school held for Year Six students allegedly to prepare them for high school. This turned out to be a film to update their sex education. It starred a laconic man with an uncombed moustache and a liberated woman with a wiggly perm, each of them wearing T-shirts patterned with gaily dancing sperm; they showed us animated pictures to explain the technicalities of intercourse. Bright colours, flashing arrows and curvaceous lines made it look pictorially wonderful.

'This is for this and this is for that,' explained the laconic man. 'This is the clitoris,' chirped the Perm, smiling brightly out of the screen at our braided eleven-year-olds. 'The clitoris is PURELY for pleasure.' The clitoris obligingly changed colour to a picnicky pink. The little girls exchanged looks. You had the impression that their idea of pleasure was making fortune-tellers from the pages of exercise books. The ones who wrote: 'You will marry a rock singer and have six children' were obviously having second thoughts.

Serenity's views when she got home were quite clear. 'I may have one very small girl baby, under anaesthetic,' she announced, 'but only if I can't be an air hostess or a vet.'

On the night I had set aside for Rash's sex education, I came prepared with a book. I had to buy it, because the one in the school library was so well-thumbed and greasy that it fell apart when I lifted it from the shelf.

Of course, Rash was younger than the others had been when I told them the facts of life, but this was typical of a third child. His curiosity would be correspondingly greater, I knew, and I wanted to have the facts at my fingertips. I would have to be thorough, accurate and unembarrassed. If that didn't work, I would treat his questions the same way my mother had treated mine. I would lie.

'Where did I come from?' he had asked and the cubs had made sure that he didn't mean Newcastle. His fascination with his own bodily bits and pieces and the years he had spent hiding under Serenity's bed (and charging his friends admission to join him) had equipped him with the knowledge that there were more differences between girls and boys than longer hair.

On the other hand, he was not as knowledgable as he liked to pretend. I realised this after our family had watched a Sunday movie in which a young couple eloped and were seen sitting up in bed together eating pizza. In the next scene the girl was pregnant. Would this have happened, Rash asked, if they'd had pepperoni instead of Hawaiian?

During my term of motherhood I felt I had experienced both extremes as a reaction to sex education. There had been misunderstanding, misery and anxiety from Turbulence, and boredom and resignation from Serenity. From Rash I expected a reasonably healthy interest.

What I didn't expect, was laughter.

I began the simple matter of reading him the facts and from the very first page, he began to chuckle.

He crowed and giggled. He roared and hooted. By the middle of the book he was hysterical. When we reached the main thrust of the story, he exploded with mirth.

Finally, when he was able to catch his breath, he looked at me with tears running down his cheeks and shared with me the reason for his hysteria. 'YOU MEAN YOU AND DAD DO THAT?' he gurgled. 'SERIOUSLY?'

'We were fairly serious at the time, if I recall,' I murmured uncomfortably.

'How often do you do it now?' He was still quivering with glee. He stuffed a hanky in his mouth to control a particularly loud giggle. 'As often as we feel like it,' I said tersely, managing with an extreme effort of will not to bring up the fact that the frequency of love making had suffered considerably at the hands . . . or actually at the throats, chests and lungs . . . of our children.

He began to whoop. 'WOW,' he chortled. 'GROSS!' And he staggered off to his room, weak at the knees with laughter.

Serenity came into the room and sat beside me on the couch. She slung a slim arm around my hunched and knotted shoulders.

'Don't worry, Mum,' she said. 'He'll have forgotten all about it by by dinner time.'

She was probably right. Any twelve-year-old who knows the clitoris is purely for pleasure is a lot wiser than her mother.

MORTGAGED Castles

Turbulence used to have beautiful teeth. Sometimes when I was lying awake at night, worrying myself sick about why my little boy was always worrying himself sick, and knowing that somehow it must have been my fault, I comforted myself with the thought that those two perfect rows of gleaming ivory castles were proof that I had done SOMETHING right.

Surely, I argued as I staggered from my bed and stumbled towards his nightly nightmare, those even white pearls were proof that while his emotions were a mess, his mouth was tidy and secure.

At least everyone says he is a very good-looking boy, I told myself, as I limped around his room, showing him yet again that there was nothing on its way out of the electricity socket to get him, and reassuring him that tomorrow was definitely not a pre-school day.

But as Turb gradually took control of his prolific anxieties, he seemed to lose control of his teeth. By second class, when he finally stopped crying at the school gate, his best pearly whites had gone to that evil scavenger, the tooth fairy, who never gives value for money. All he had to show for it were a few miserable twenty cent pieces and some cavernous gaps. (Everyone Else's Tooth Fairy gives gold!) With the disappearance of his first teeth, his rare but wonderful smile went too.

During primary school, when he finally conquered his separation anxiety and could even walk past a power point without shuddering, many new teeth had moved in. Now he smiled much more often. But the effect was not the same.

These were foreign teeth, uninvited refugees from some unknown land of giants, speckled, spotty and far too big for the limited amount of vacant space available to them. Yet the invasion continued. The gums swelled, the lips ran riot around them and it became obvious even to a woman with neither a dental degree nor a designer wardrobe (our dentist has both) that these refugees would keep coming until the place they wished to call their own was no longer recognisable as the sweet mouth of a handsome young boy.

The simplest solution, pointed out his grandmother, was the old-fashioned one of removing a few of the biggest troublemakers by force. But this is not an option in the nineties. These days, teeth have rights. There may be too many of them, but each one is strong and healthy. Cleaned day and night, coated with fluoride and sealed against decay by our dentist who travels the long distance to our suburb every day to save the smiles of children like Turbulence, these teeth will be around for a lifetime. You can't cut down a good tooth in its prime, she explained, simply because there's nowhere for it to go.

Instead, our dentist suggested we should put the rebels behind metal wires and wait for them to fall into line. In other words, she sent us to see an orthodontist.

It was just our luck to get one who had finished restoring the beach mansion, had bought his jacuzzi and had paid off the cars. Quite simply, he didn't need the money. He told us that as Turbulence grew, space would be created. The teeth would probably sort themselves out. In the meantime, Turb could still eat and smile and speak, so there was probably no need for him to wear braces.

Relief shot through my veins as if I had been injected by a mad scientist with a hypodermic full of joy. It was going to be all right. We wouldn't have to take out the new mortgage or give up five years of holidays at the beach. And Turb's teeth would be all right. In time.

'The only reason you, as his parent, might want to put him into braces,' murmured the orthodontist, picking some floss from his soft leather jacket, 'would be to give him a perfect smile.'

The gratitude slipped from my face. The joy froze in my veins. What sort of choice is that? screamed my subconscious, that same subconscious which had agreed with me that once, long ago, I had done something right. How can a mother be expected to choose between restoring her first-born's former beauty and years of wires and debt?

I could have said that I didn't want Turb to look like a Ken doll. I could have said that irregular teeth gave a face character. I could have lied.

As we walked slowly to the car, Turb hauled his lips back into a smile which revealed crowds of teeth, scrambling for a hold. It was a scene similar to the ones you see in tourist brochures of whitewashed villages in Greece.

'If we're going to do it, Mum,' he said cheerfully, 'let's do it now before I get old enough to start kissing.'

I took him home and made him sit in front of an electricity socket while I thought it over.

THE GOOD Mother

It was the sight of Charmaine shampooing her garage door that made me realise how slack I have become about being a good wife and mother.

Never in my life have I shampooed my garage door. I haven't even wiped it over. Once I hosed it down, but that was after Rash and his friends had used it as a target for rotten peaches practice.

Charmaine, who lives over the road, also winds up her garden hose each time she has used it and shines the tap and washes both the family cars every Saturday. I can't help admiring her, while at the same time making a mental note to look up the date of the next Cubs' Community Car Wash.

Charmaine is definitely a Good Wife and Mother and so is Wendy, who washes her walls once a week. I try not to wonder why she would do that. What can possibly happen to walls that they need such regular scrubbing? True, walls are painted pastel and easily marked. But by their nature, walls are vertical. It's hard to get grot to stick to them. It's harder still imagining Wendy's two slight and silent daughters indulging in weekly graffiti sessions, equipped with textas, spaghetti sauce or the sort of substances that I do find on my own walls at intermittent, but not weekly, intervals.

I know a lot of Good Wives and Mothers who, even when they go out to work, find enough time to do things which take up the treasured hours that I allocate to sleeping, reading, writing, eating or talking about my kids over a cappuccino.

There's Camilla who composts (Rash brought home a worm farm from cubs but they all became brain damaged after we fed them leftover salmon dip) and Glenda who grows her own herbs (but it's so cold going out into the garden at tea time and the jars are easier to open). Rowena actually repots her plants when they get too big instead of going to the nursery and getting new ones. Tessa makes tea with real leaves. Belinda bakes her own bread and makes birthday cakes shaped like rockets and retrievers.

Then there are the polishers. Pamela polishes her front steps. Prudence polishes the leaves of her indoor plants until she can see her face in them. (I prefer mirrors but only because I've never looked good in green.) Penny shines her children's shoes with real polish, out of those little flat tins that you can never open.

The only time I've ever substituted effort for convenience is when I made my own playdough from flour and water and cream of tartar. It was a magnificent success, being both malleable and edible and it lasted for so long the kids got sick of playing with it. When I boasted to a friend she said: 'Couldn't you get it at the shop?'

It was Greta who finally roused me to action. Greta doesn't bake or garden or sew all her children's concert costumes or make foot mats from thinning bath towels.

But Greta gets up in the morning.

Greta rises at five-thirty a.m. and has tea and toast with her eldest son before he goes to his very distant school. She says they both enjoy the time together. This, at least, I could understand.

So this morning I got up at seven a.m. instead of snuggling in for a bit more bliss and staggered out to spend time with Turbulence and Serenity.

Turb was in the toilet and apparently unlikely to emerge for quite some time. I found Serenity in her room, clutching handfuls of mousse. 'I thought I would have breakfast with you,' I said, smiling through crusty eyes. She looked surprised. 'I've had it,' she said. 'I eat my toast at my desk while I colour in my title pages.'

I took a deeply guilty breath. 'It would be nice to have a little chat before you disappear for the day,' I said. So she came out, and waited patiently while I jiggled my tea bag.

I looked at her for a while over my mug. Serenity looked at the sticky bench top and then up at the mould-spotted ceiling where a spider was busily spinning its web around a hanging plant with dull leaves which needed repotting.

'There's jam on your jumper,' I said. 'Your blouse collar is all rucked up and your hair needs washing.'

'I have to leave in five minutes,' said Serenity. 'Can I go back to my room now?'

Today, after I've driven Rash to school I'm going to the hardware store to buy that special shampoo for garage doors. I might even get some conditioner as well.

PUBERTY Bites

'I want a divorce,' he said, frowning hard at his feet as he loomed over me in my favourite chair.

For a second or so, I wanted to laugh with disbelief. Then, as I realised he was serious, my stomach cramped and my eyes began to sting.

How could he dare to suggest such a thing, after everything I had done for him? I'd washed his clothes, cooked his food, cleaned up after him, given him the best years of my life. I'd cried for him and cheered for him. If not for him, I would still have a career, a figure, a healthy bank balance.

With a massive effort, achieved not by will but by clenching my teeth tightly and squeezing my lips together with my fingers, I managed not to say any of this. I took a deep breath.

'Turbulence,' I said slowly, 'you're only a kid. Who do you want to get a divorce FROM?'

'All of you,' he said simply. 'This family. I don't feel good any more and it's all your fault.'

Turbulence was hot. His face was red, his T-shirt was steaming and had suddenly become too small. Little puffs of hot air rose from his sweaty head. As he turned away angrily and stomped off, his shoelaces snaked behind him in a dumb challenge to my authority. I knew things were bad if Turb, of all people, wasn't bothering to neatly tie his sneakers.

I looked at his retreating legs. They seemed to have exploded overnight. They were covered in curly down. They were a danger to his shorts.

Turbulence was getting bigger, angrier, hairier and hotter even as I watched him go.

Turbulence had become an adolescent.

When did it happen? When did my tiny, tidy, docile, sweet-smelling little pup turn into a snarling, dissatisfied whelp?

Of course we had noticed some changes coming. We'd bought bigger clothes and deodorant and even wondered about razor blades. But while his body was changing gradually, until very recently his personality had remained the same. He was still clean, neat, affectionate and anxious to keep all the rules.

'Nobody in this house cares about my life!' he suddenly roared over his shoulder at nobody in particular. 'We haven't got a pool, like normal people. We don't live near the beach like they do in 'Baywatch' or 'Home and Away'. Nitty's up in YOUR bathroom using up all the shower water. Rash has been in the bath with forty-five plastic power rangers and a golf stick for about a MONTH! Dad won't let ME have a bath unless I get WASHED in it!'

'Don't call Serenity Nitty,' I said faintly. He had broken the family rule about cruel nicknames. 'You can get some water from the laundry if you're desperate to cool down.'

'Great,' bellowed Turb. 'My mates have pools, my brother lives permanently in the bath and I get to do laps in a pink plastic laundry tub.'

His sarcasm tore at my conscience. I knew he'd learned how to do it entirely from me.

'It's not my fault there's a drought!' I called after him. 'It seems pretty stupid that you suddenly want to leave us all just because right at this minute there is no suitably vast container of water for you to get into!'

'That's right!' screamed Turb from the hall, but suddenly the scream turned into a deep roar and the voice was no longer that of a cub but that of a Lion King. 'Tell me how fat I am! Tell me I'm stupid! Thanks heaps!'

The injustice of these accusations clogged my throat. I had NOT said he was fat. The guilt hurt my chest. WHY hadn't we saved enough for a pool? Or better still, a house beside the beach? The pain cramped my stomach. My baby boy's cheerful chirrupy voice was suddenly as deep as his father's.

I wanted to bellow at him that he was being outrageously unreasonable and unfair to us all.

I wanted to bound after him and hold him tightly to stop him from growing up and out and away from me.

Instead I went back into the kitchen and wiped my eyes on a tea towel. Then I looked in the secret spot at the back of the fridge where I hide my premenstrual Mars bars.

I took one into his room with a nice cold drink.

'Have a pimple,' I said.

His eyes lit up. 'Cool!' said Turbulence and he almost smiled. He peeled off the wrapper, folded it neatly and put it in his bin. Then he broke it in two and offered the second half to me.

'So that's that,' I thought with relief as we chewed silently together.

But of course, it was only the beginning.

AN Ancient Art

Her eyes were popping, her face was strained and her small frame was hunched uncomfortably into the corner of my couch, but her tiny jaw was set.

'No thankyou, Aunty Fran,' she said grimly. 'I DON'T want to go to the toilet.'

I was baby-sitting my little niece, Token, who is about halfway though her toilet training program. The only child of a mother who is slicing through the glass ceiling with barely a scratch, and a father who is a better mother than most women will ever be, Token is not the textbook tot her parents had every right to expect. She has no interest in food, she finds people, especially adult relatives, a bore and she is particularly offended by authority. At two, she is still in double O fittings, yet she has the vocabulary of a barrister and the personality of a menopausal woman.

Toilet training Token was never going to be easy. What is making it even more difficult for her devoted Dad is that he has so efficiently changed her nappy at the first sign of damp for the duration of her life to date that she is unaware that having her nether regions wrapped in disposable padding holds any disadvantages.

When luck finally struck and she performed while sitting on her sleek designer potty chair, she was so appalled at the thought that such gross material had come from her own small sweet body that she screamed for an hour and refused to open her bowels for the following week.

Inevitably the textbooks were laid aside and her parents resorted to bribery.

We all go that way in the end.

We successfully bribed Turbulence to go to school every day. We told him that each time he made it through until three o'clock without crying or getting a stomach cramp he could go without broccoli or peas for dinner. Years later we tried the same thing with piano practice. For every day he practised without complaining, he could grow his hair. In both cases it worked. The lack of greens did not seem to affect his development. He passed his music exams, with his rat's tail tickling the top of his bottom and the day after he got his results I hauled him off to the hairdresser. (He never touched the piano again. On the other hand, he never grew his hair again either.)

We bribed Serenity to clean her room. We offered her a hot dog for every time she contributed a complete sentence to our dinner table conversation. We gave her paints and pencils and iridescent textas in return for picking up the bath mat, keeping her roller blades out of the hall and putting her craft clippings into her bin.

Because bribery becomes easier once you've been seduced by its effectiveness, we began bribing Rash at a very early age and by then we were in a position to dispense with the soft stuff and offer hard cash. We bribed him to get up in the morning, to go to bed at night, to eat vegetables, to wash, to clean his teeth, to JUST ONCE remember what he needed to take to school, to do his chores, to eat with his mouth closed, to speak with his mouth open, to stop throwing balls in the house, to stop throwing bats in the house, to point his guns at kneecaps only, to practise his piano, to stop practising his trumpet. If Rash had ever done the things we bribed him to do, he would now be wealthy enough to invest in Surfers Paradise real estate and we would be homeless and on the street. Fortunately — or unfortunately, depending on your point of view — Rash's behaviour is beyond bribery. He so rarely does anything he's told that the family finances are still safe with us.

So when Token refused to use her potty I knew exactly what to do. First, having triumphed over the bladders of my own three children, I did the obvious. I turned on a tap. Then, whistling a little tune about rain falling down, I pulled a box of smarties out of the pantry and placed them on the bench.

I didn't even have to speak. After summing up the situation, Token disappeared into the bathroom. A few minutes later, she called me in. Feeling smug, I smiled around the bathroom door.

'Now don't say anything, please, Aunty Fran,' said Token sternly, pulling up pants no larger than a ladies handkerchief. 'Don't say: "WHAT a good girl". Don't hug. Don't scream. Don't make your mouth into a circle and don't put your eyebrows up high.

'And don't clap,' she added, as I stood there, speechless, blank-faced and obedient.

'Just give me the smarties,' said Token, and she held out her tiny hand.

Now THERE's a girl who understands that bribery is an art!

IT'S Snow Contest

She pursed her sun-blocked lips, narrowed her eyes behind trendy sunglasses and tapped her foot in its enormous boot. 'What was the point in coming all this way if you're just going to stand there and cry?' she asked sensibly.

'I'm not crying,' I said pathetically. 'Some snow flew into my eye. I might have to go to the Ladies to get it out.'

'For Heaven's sake, Mum,' said Serenity, in exasperation. 'It's not even snowing. And you've been in the Ladies for the past fifty minutes. Are you coming skiing or not?'

That's the trouble with adolescent girls. Just because they can skate and roller blade and ride a bike and you can't, just because they look fabulous in a skin-tight ski suit and a beanie, whereas you bear a frightening resemblance to a teapot on steroids, just because they learned to ski in the twenty minutes it took you to learn how to adjust the boots, they think they suddenly outrank you. They start giving orders.

They make ridiculous statements like: 'You've paid for a lesson, so you might as well have it' and 'the exercise will do you good' and 'you'll never know if you can do it if you don't have a go'.

To me, the idea of skiing has always been right up there with abseiling, giving birth under water and leg waxing — I'm glad it's available to those who want it but I'm happy down here where it's flat, dry and just a little fuzzy.

It was a moment of pure horror when Serenity's latest best friend, a terrifyingly multi-talented only child, invited us all to join her family for a skiing weekend.

We are a beach family, I told Serenity, hopefully. We'd rather be hot than cold. We prefer sand to snow. We like horizontal relaxation.

But they were offering free accommodation — and we had always promised to show the children snow.

I discovered that walking on snow is a bit harder than walking on sand — but not much. Learning to ski is slightly more difficult than learning to swim — but not much. Hurtling downhill while trying to remain upright is more terrifying than being swept out to sea while keeping your head above water — but not much.

Falling in snow hurts less than being dumped by a wave — but not enough for it to matter.

In other words, apart from the cost, being at the snow was not all that different to being at the beach. Instead of sweeping views of the ocean we had sweeping views of white crystal slopes. Instead of gorgeous young people with broad brown shoulders and fluoro G-strings there were gorgeous young people with broad shoulders and skin-tight fluoro snow suits.

Instead of undernourished life-savers in sensible jerseys with nut brown faces, zinced lips and sunnies, there were undernourished ski instructors in uniform parkas, with nut brown faces, zinced lips and sunnies.

Instead of seasoned surfers whirling up in a flurry of foam and staring out to sea in search of the perfect wave there were seasoned skiers whirling up in a flurry of snow and staring at the horizon in search of the perfect run.

We had only been at the snow for a morning before these men of action were joined by a newcomer. Rash, who before that day had never even touched his toe to a ski, had found a new role to play in a life already crammed with parts (most of them, sooner or later, broken parts).

'You ought to try it, Mum,' he shouted, whirling up in a flurry of snow on the first afternoon. 'Come on down!'

At the edge of the snowfields young parents still nagged young children. 'What was the point of us coming if you're not even going to TRY to ski/swim?'

Finally, there were the same self-centred, middle-sized kids that you find at the beach.

'Justin, keep to the edge of the slope/flags or you'll run into someone with your board/toboggan. Oh JUSTIN! I'm sorry, Madam. I don't think he realised you were actually moving.'

'That's okay,' I said, smiling up at her with just the same expression I wore when I had been ploughed down by a boogy board in the surf. The only difference was that this time I couldn't get up.

'Would you mind calling my daughter?' I asked politely. 'I think it's time she taught me how to take off my skis.'

It had taken me many patient months to show Serenity how to tie her shoelaces. The way I saw it, she owed me one.

And I WASN'T crying!

ROUGH Love

If spring is the season of the year when most people cast themselves into the sea of love, then autumn must be the season when the ocean becomes rough and full of rips.

At least that's how is seems here at No. 1 Frustration Close.

The tide started turning when Rash arrived at school to be told by a bunch of braided hussies that last term's love of his life had thrown him over for the tiny but apparently terrifically attractive tuba player in the school band.

Well, what they actually said to him was: 'You're dropped.' Being 'dropped' has been a devastating experience for a boy who is first trumpet, handball champion, computer monitor, swimming star and life support to the school cricket team. It has badly affected his ultra-cool image and has even slightly dented his previously impenetrable self-esteem.

Typically, Rash blames his father, who came to pick him up from the last school disco.

It seems Rash was slow dancing with little Curva Cummings, the junior netball champion, when the Good Husband appeared in the doorway of the hall and ordered Rash to leave right away. The slap of our son's sneakers on the school cement had barely faded from earshot before Tim the tuba player stepped in to take his place.

'It's pretty disgusting that I have to look like a fool just because Dad decided to park in a No Standing zone,' grumbled Rash when he got home with a face as red as a traffic light.

'Well you are too young to be slow dancing with one girl anyway,' I said. 'You should be friends with lots of girls.'

'I was,' said Rash, looking surprised. Serenity explained to me that slow dancing with Curva would actually have involved slow dancing in a line of boys with an even longer line of girls.

I was relieved to hear that he hadn't been physically torn from Curva's sparrow-like arms. 'So you weren't actually touching at the time?' I asked.

'Of COURSE not,' he said. 'How disgusting.'

Turbulence of course has never had a problem with girls because he has always been too worried about himself to notice they exist. Now that puberty has struck, however, the girls are noticing HIM. As a matter of fact, Turbulence has always been a rather beautiful boy. When he was still in the hospital a tactful and now former friend looked at our baby son and then at the Good Husband and me and asked: 'How could two people who look like you have produced something as gorgeous as THAT?'

Nothing much has changed. As a result of which, the phone never stops ringing. Girls from school, girls from the pool, girls from the back pew at church, girls from the supermarket checkout — girls whom Serenity and I can identify only as 'The Skirt', 'The Legs', or 'The Freckle' – keep Turb engaged in prolonged conversations which cut the rest of the family off from telecommunication with the free world.

Dinner time calls have a disastrous effect on my husband's digestion. What the Good Husband is most concerned about, apart from the time it takes Turb to identify the female on the other end of the line, is the way he ends each call. 'Gotta go,' he always says. 'Have a good one.'

'Have a good WHAT?' the Good Husband will ask me with potato in his mouth and panic in his eye, and our minds mutually boggle.

The fact that GH and I still do some things together, even if it's only boggling, is a relief to Serenity. She is concerned about relationships on a larger scale.

'Everyone's getting divorced,' she sighed at the dinner table. 'I don't understand why people get married if they are going to break up in the end.'

I tried to point out that despite the depressing statistics, of all the people we knew, only two were divorced. 'And,' said her father reassuringly, 'they are the two happiest people we know.'

'I still don't understand,' said Serenity unhappily. 'If they start off loving each other, why do they change their minds?'

Turbulence was on the phone but Rash, with the experience of his own recent separation, took it upon himself to explain the facts of life to his older sister.

'When people get married they go down the aisle to the priest who makes them man and wife,' he said. 'To get divorced, they have to go all the way back up the aisle, walking BACKWARDS.

'Obviously,' he went on, as we absorbed this information, 'it's easier to stay married and keep walking forwards. But there will always be some people who decide they'll have a better time doing it the other way.'

The GH looked at me and opened his mouth but I was already out of my chair and nearly to the door.

'Gotta go,' I said. 'Have a good one.'

THE FAKE Escape

I am leaving my children.

My time is up. My moment has arrived. After fifteen years of permanent parenting, I am going to set myself free.

Years ago, when my skin was still as smooth as a pillow slip before it hits the spin drier and when I spent my money only on me, way back when weariness and exhaustion were simply the signs of a sizzling Saturday night, I went on a working holiday abroad.

Now I'm returning. On the pretext of working on some of my More Serious Stories I am going to visit old friends and old places. I may even see the seamy pub where I met the Good Husband, the callow Irish youth who eventually made this life of mine (my children, my house, my wobbly word processor and therefore even this book) a stark reality.

Of course it's only a fake escape. I'm coming back. Yet for four whole weeks I will not mark a sum, peel an apple or sort a sock. For twenty-eight days I will not iron a shirt, stitch on a button, mash a potato, scrub a shin pad, rinse a flipper, locate a school hat, peel a bandaid, or gladwrap a lunch.

I will not listen to trumpet or piano practice. I will not soak a grass stain nor deal tenderly with a T-shirt which cost more than my wedding ring and must always be separately washed and ironed on the wrong side. My nostrils will not be assailed by the smell of pool chlorine, nor my ears with the guilt-inducing jibes of cursing coaches. The only heavy metal I will hear will be the latches locking on my suitcase.

I will not drive ANYONE ANYWHERE.

I can't wait.

'Go for it,' shout my loyal and long-standing friends. They understand. They would gladly kill me. Instead they are taking it in turns to mind Rash after school. Some are rearranging their furniture to accommodate his weapon collection. That's friendship.

Turbulence of course, is worried. Inevitably, his concern is less about the possibility of my plane crashing into the sea at 11,000 feet than about the problem of who will wash and properly iron his white jeans. If he has to go somewhere important while I am in England, who will drive him? Who will check the back view of his hair? Who will prepare the Panadol when he's upset? Who will talk to him about his Trouble of the Week?

Who indeed?

Serenity is worried too. People keep assuring me in her hearing that now that my daughter is old enough to help around the house, my absence will hardly be noticed.

What Serenity had not noticed until they mentioned it, however, was that she was old enough to help around the house. Asked to have a practice run, she staggers through the kitchen door, wheezing with the effort of carrying a plastic basket of socks, and collapses in the TV room for half an hour to recover her strength. At the suggestion that she should actually sort and fold the socks, her eyes dilate and a hurt and suffering pain appears on her brow. She struggles to her feet, suddenly remembering homework.

Rash is ecstatic. He has found a calendar and is marking off the days. Dancing before his eyes is an orgy of glorious bath-free weeks, in which neither homework, vegetables, tooth-brush, comb, nor bedtime will be inflicted upon him. He fantasises about four-hour sessions on the Sega, lollies in the lounge room and chocolate ice blocks on the trampoline. He keeps re-running the first thirty minutes of *Home Alone* and laughing crazily.

As long as I make a simple list, the children's father assures me, everything will be taken care of. But there are some things you can't cover with a list. Like illness.

'What if they get sick and call out to you in the night?' I ask the Good Husband. He looks astonished.

'Do they REALLY do that?' he asks, with a lilting laugh.

'And what were you planning to do about meals?' I ask him nervously. I don't relish the prospect of cooking twenty-eight dinners for the freezer.

He lowers his eyes to hide his confusion. When he looks at me again he is wearing the same expression I'd seen on Turbulence's face when he asked me why Santa had stopped leaving him so many presents once he turned fourteen. 'Um, I'll be the one to be feeding them, will I?' asks GH.

'Three times a day,' I say. 'Breakfast, lunch, dinner. Like in those TV commercials they put on with the football.'

'We could go to Mackers!' cries Rash.

'Surely not every night,' I say coldly.

'Every second night,' says Turbulence thoughtfully. 'On the alternate nights we could buy pizza.'

I laugh scornfully. The GH laughs too.

But they probably will.

BACK TO Basics

I didn't want to write about my overseas adventure . . . or rather, its effect on my children . . . until I had got everything into perspective.

Before leaping into purple prose to describe the incredibly tidy sight of my home under the efficiently quiet control of the Good Husband and his little people, I wanted to see if it would last.

After all, I told myself, there is no reason to depress all my readers for nothing. There is no reason to persuade them into thinking that Turbulence, Serenity and Rash, not to mention their father, turned over the crispest and whitest new leaf possible while I was away — not if there's a strong possibility of the leaf lazily flipping backwards within days of my return.

Okay, so during my four weeks away, Rash was hired out as cheap entertainment to friends. That made life easier for the ones left behind. But even so, they still had to eat. They still had to get to school. They still had to find enough of their bed to sleep in every night. They still had to wear clothes and if there were none of these left in their cupboards, presumably they still had to wash and iron them.

The first thing I noticed when I returned was the extreme tidiness of the home. Nothing was out of place. The chairs and coffee tables were at just the right angle to each other. The dining table was bare of homework, school notes and plate stains. The beds were bereft of their normal loads of clothing. The dead flowers, now four weeks old, stood brown and erect in their vases, their fallen petals neatly swept away.

But I didn't want to write about it in case the kids had just done it for effect. It might have been one of those last minute panic efforts, the kind you have when you see visitors' cars cruising up the driveway and you shove everything into the nearest cupboards, grubby bras into saucepans, homework sheets under the breadboard, bundles of unironed shirts into the video cabinet.

The next thing I became aware of, because they couldn't wait to tell me, was that Serenity had learned to cook. Desperate for ordinary meat and potato type food after a fortnight of pizzas and McDonalds, she had learned how to place pre-crumbed chicken fillets on a tray, leave them in the oven for forty-five minutes, remove them and put them on plates!

She had also learned how to put broccoli in a dish and press a microwave button to produce steamed vegetables. She had even washed the new potatoes and done the same to them.

As for salads, cutting and scraping salad ingredients had turned out to be closely aligned with art and craft . . . it's just that you ate the result instead of standing it on the windowsill for five years. Serenity's salads, they told me, were without peer!

But I didn't want to write about it until I was sure that Serenity would continue to cut up cucumbers after I returned. I wasn't sure whether she would still volunteer to work with chicken and broccoli, once her beloved mother was there to fiddle with fettucini, pulverise pumpkin and scrape the skin of cheap, elderly, unwashed spuds, the like of which Serenity preferred not to handle.

Meanwhile, Turbulence was bursting with pride at the fact that he had taught himself to iron. This should have come as no surprise. After all, Turbulence has spent most of his life attempting to find a smooth and uncreased path through the troubled times fate has set before him. Little wonder then that he enjoyed plunging a steaming iron over the wrinkled shirts and flattening the lumpy seams of jeans.

I didn't want to write about it before I was certain that Turb's ironing efforts weren't just a therapeutic activity designed to pass the time while he gritted his teeth and tried to survive the ghastliness of his mother's absence and the inevitable but unendurable change in the regular routine of his regular, routine little life.

Before putting it down on paper, I wanted to see if it would all last . . . the tidiness, the cooking, the ironing and the washing. ('Right,' trilled the GH, 'we're doing a load of darks and coloureds, so hurry up because the cycle's starting NOW'.) How enduring, I wondered, was the overwhelming affection and consideration which saw me surrounded by such smiling faces and attentive hands, on that first day when I walked back through the door?

I didn't want to depress you all with my idyllic new situation if it wasn't going to be a permanent thing. I know you'll think I'm silly, but I just had the vaguest feeling that maybe it wouldn't last.

And I was thinking, as I pulled one of Serenity's grubby bras out of a saucepan this morning, and retrieved a crumpled shirt from the video cabinet, that it's lucky I postponed this article.

Because I was right. And it didn't.

GOING Green

A golden dollop of margarine melted softly into the creamy potato. The chicken was baked to tender perfection. The carrots glowed beneath their honeyed glaze. The spinach shone. The tiny bouquets of broccoli were a deep, glimmering, green. I slid the plates on to the table with a self-satisfied smile. I had excelled myself.

'Yuck,' said Rash, and his mouth turned down with disgust. 'I hate this green stuff.'

'Why can't we have salad?' asked Serenity, scowling. 'Everyone else's mother gives them salad and it's better for you. Look at all this revolting margerine. It's pure fat, you know.'

'I can't eat spinach,' said Turbulence. 'Bits of it get stuck in my braces. And if this is chicken, I hope it's the kind that saw daylight before it died.'

When my children were very small I had a theory that either your children were good sleepers or they were good eaters. No mother should be greedy enough to expect both.

Mine were good sleepers. Well, the first two were. And although it always took forever to get them to digest anything that looked as if it might even be vaguely nutritious, I remained optimistic. When they were older, they would come to share my love of good food. In the meantime, at least I was pushing the purée through their clamped lips with the patience made possible by an uninterrupted night's sleep.

These days they sleep a lot less and eat a lot more. But my optimism has not been rewarded. Meal times are still a nightmare.

First there is the issue of their manners which is too depressing to write about at all. (But why DO we use our fork in the left hand and load it upside down?) Then, despite all their health education, not to mention years of nutritional nagging, there is the sad fact that all three of them have a serious attitude problem about consuming anything that's good for them.

Particularly if it's green.

Oh, Serenity says she likes salad. What she means is that she likes a sliver of lettuce, a slice of celery, a heap of tinned pineapple and a hunk of high-fat cheese, with the lot blanketed pinkly in thousand island dressing.

Because of his alarming and long established obedience, Turbulence will now eat his vegetables. But he will cut his greens into tiny slices and mash them into mounds of potato rather than taint his taste buds with the flavour of health. And since the braces have been clamped to his ivories he has had the perfect excuse to avoid almost every form of protein.

(I am fascinated by the fact that while Turbulence's teeth can no longer chomp chops, they can still cope with chocolate. He tells me I could not possibly understand how braced teeth wobble and sway when they come into contact with certain foods . . . all of them nutritious, most of them green.)

Rash was born allergic to almost everything that's good for other people, but particularly to greens. Whenever he gets a rash, a cold or a wheeze, he is quick to point out that he has almost always been eating some form of green vegetable the night before.

To no avail do I limit his serving to the smallest piece of broccoli, a teaspoon of peas, or a sprout the size of a pimple. If it's green, it's ghastly. He moves it around his plate, he builds it into towers and covers it with crusts, he drowns it in tomato sauce and hopes I won't notice.

I notice. I spent ten years camouflaging my cabbage. I've been there.

Carrots bump into his cheek, peas make him bite his tongue. Potatoes make him wretch. The only meat that doesn't make his jaw tired from chewing is the beef inside a bought burger.

Rash is not entirely unappreciative of my culinary skills. He is quick to admire the way I can tear open a box of nuggets and dump them on an oven tray. And he says I dial a pizza with real flair.

Which brings us to the problem of eating out.

Visiting a restaurant can hardly be considered a treat when the first thing they ask the waitress is whether she can do cheese and peanut butter sandwiches exactly the same as the ones Mum makes at home. Nothing on the 'mains' menu ever suits them — there's a danger that something on there may be good for them, even though none of the meals are anything like the ones they get at home. You don't know what this foreign food might do to them — in fact for my children, stranger danger applies mainly to eating out.

When they were little we were reduced to ordering a small plate of chips for them to play with while we tried to enjoy our meal. Now that Turbulence and Serenity are in their teens, we have to order a much larger plate.

My friend Moana's daughter won't go to bed at night without her treat of a stick of celery and a glass of milk. (Needless to say, this child did not sleep through the night until she was three.) Even so, Moana tells me that my children's attitude to vegetables is my own fault. She says I should have convinced them that eating nutritious food was a treat rather than a hardship.

I thought back to when my children could neither walk nor talk nor comprehend much at all. I remembered how I used to wave spoons full of puréed vegetables in front of their faces, making loud smacking noises with my lips, drooling, moaning in ecstasy, and doing aeroplane approaches for an hour at a time until I finally got just a little bit of nutrition through their damp pink lips.

I remembered how they spat it out.

Whether or not I'm to blame, all I can do is keep making wholesome meals and reminding them every evening that if they don't eat their vegetables, their protein, their fruit and their crusts, they'll never grow up to be big, strong and healthy children.

If they weren't growing up so big and strong and healthy — and if their hair wasn't quite so curly — I might have more success.

GREAT Expectations

Do you know what frustrates me most about being a mother? It's the way nothing, NOTHING ever turns out the way you expect it to.

Take childbirth, for instance. Of course we know it's going to hurt. When all the exercise classes are over, when we've read all the books and seen the video and watched the ladies writhing in the soaps, we know we're in for a dose of natural agony. But we also know that the pain lasts a day, usually less, and is almost instantly forgotten. And at the end of that day we will have a beautiful bundle of joy to show for it.

Nobody talks about stitches! Nobody mentions how the issue of whether the nurses can find you an air pillow to sit on before the visitors arrive is only marginally less important than whether your baby has eleven toes. Nobody warns you that in those frantic, harried, exhausting days when you first take your new baby home, you have to find time to soak your tail in a salts bath two or three times a day or die in the attempt. And after giving birth to a child so large that every time you see a sailing schooner in a glass bottle you flinch, sooner or later you actually have to start going to the toilet again. Nobody even hints about THAT.

Is it just me or do most women produce children who break every rule in all the books I read and write for? I mean, I remember looking forward to answering all the questions Turbulence was going to heap upon me when he learned to talk. He would be a little sponge and I would fill him with wisdom.

As far as I recall, Turb only ever asked one question in the first five years of his life. It was: 'Will it hurt me?' There were variations, such as 'will it stop?' and 'will it come back?' but I'm sure you get the drift. It wasn't the sort of material that sent either of us rushing to the encyclopaedia to enrich our knowledge.

Then there was the second child theory. Serenity would be a terror; her arrival would disrupt Turbulence's routines completely. In fact, Serenity lay in her bouncer for nine months staring intelligently at the ceiling and occasionally consulting her hands. Turbulence continued to worry about the world and everything in it which related to him.

Nothing much has changed. Even being a middle child has not transformed Serenity into a persecuted mess. And if the back of her head is a little flat from all those months in the bouncer, her mane of thick curls disguises it. Need I add that she has never eaten a crust in her life?

Unlike our other two children, Rash is relatively normal. At last I was blessed with a child who refused to sleep through the night, walked before he was two, asked a thousand questions a day (it's an unfortunate fact of life that by then my enthusiasm had gone off the boil) and required constant entertainment. Rash's presence in the family turned me into a nag. Yet nothing I nag him about ever comes off.

'If you don't clean your teeth they'll decay,' I say. He forgets most nights and the dentist congratulates him every six months on his gleaming ivories. 'If you don't take your puffers you'll get asthma,' I say. So the day he forgets his puffers he wins every race. 'If you insult your friends that way you'll end up a very lonely little boy,' I mutter. He continues to talk to his friends as if they were head lice and they continue to queue for his favours. 'If you're late for cubs every week they'll think you are unreliable,' I warn. So they make him a Sixer. 'If you write out your spelling words you won't get them wrong,' I announce. But he does.

'If you don't eat your vegetables you'll get sick,' I threaten. Now here's a twist. Rash doesn't eat properly and he does get sick. So he starts eating up all his greens and hey! He gets sick twice as often!

Perhaps there's a reason why I have been blessed with a family who are exceptions to every proven theory about child raising. Perhaps my failures are meant to cheer the rest of you up. I hope it's working. Because here at No. 1 Frustration Close, I'm feeling pretty silly.

WHEN 'P' MEANS Free

Now you see it, now you don't. What's mine is his, what's his used to be mine but is now almost never available when I need it. Is this a riddle? Not for the parents of seventeen-year-old children. They know already that I'm talking about my car.

There are many well-dissected issues which trip up parents just past the halfway post of life. There's the male mid-life crisis, there's menopause, there's the grandparents getting giddy, there's superannuation or lack of it, there's cholesterol, there's the way your face falls forward in folds whenever you bend over. And of course there are adolescent children and the risk that your biggest investment in terms of time, affection and finance, might be written off due to seduction by drugs, alcohol or pretty girls.

But as well prepared for trouble as most parents have become, how many of us realise the impact that a teenager with a driver's licence will have on the family?

Learners are bad enough. Suddenly, nothing in the household takes priority over driving lessons. You may be straight out of the shower wearing nothing but your no-frills undies and your no-frizz perm but the Learner will burst into your bathroom to demand that you help him with hill starts. You may be just home from an exhausting day of balancing other men's millions, looking forward to a meal and a bit of teev, and the Learner will not understand why you're not prepared to slide over into the passenger seat and plunge back into the traffic.

You've spent the first four years or so of their puberty watching them assume the escape position whenever you want to speak to them but with Learners all that changes. They're beside you constantly, hanging around the kitchen bench, holding up the doorways, interrupting, nagging, cajoling, planning, pleading for your keys — pining for their Ps.

The American humorist Erma Bombeck once described eternity as a Christmas ham. I disagree. I believe Eternity can most accurately be defined as sitting beside a seventeen-year-old who is perfecting a reverse park.

In the last twelve months, 62,000 seventeen-year-olds in my state were granted drivers licences. But having their P plates doesn't just mean they can drive. For young men in particular, the achievement marks the beginning of freedom. 'Total mobility and participation in the adult world are suddenly possible,' says Steve Biddulph in his book *Manhood* (Finch), in which he describes getting a licence as a form of modern initiation.

Biddulph suggests that this important step would benefit from an adult dinner with parents and older relatives 'to imbue the moment with both congratulation and gravity'.

'YES!' shrieked Turbulence as he leapt through the doors of the motor registry and raced to replace his Ls with the red and white plates which were about to shoot my vehicle's petrol consumption to an all-time high.

'COOL!' bellowed our gravel-voiced baby boy as he turned his hat backwards, gunned the motor and dropped me home before roaring off to collect all his friends. They were planning to imbue the moment with both congratulation and joyful hysteria.

I wobbled unsteadily into my house. My brake foot had gone into spasm again. I was alone, trapped in the suburbs without a vehicle. The last time I was in this situation I had been so busy with babies and nappy rash that I hadn't cared. Besides, back then I knew how to catch a bus. Now, by setting my fledgling free, I had become, albeit temporarily, a prisoner in my own nest.

Apart from that, the personality change which had begun with the first sign of fuzz on Turb's satin cheek seemed now to be complete. The Boy Who Worried seemed to have been taken over by The Boy Who Drove. I would not have been all that surprised if his head had turned backwards with his hat and green stuff had poured from his grinning mouth. To my amazement, after years of yearning for the moment when my eldest child finally found happiness, I wasn't sure I liked it.

In the first six weeks, teenage P-platers want to drive EVERYWHERE. They are even willing to transport their siblings to all those extracurricular activities which drive (pardon the pun) most parents mad. You are torn between delight at being relieved from the tedious taxi runs and terrific tension as you accept that not only are the car and the P-plater out of your sight and out of your control, the rest of your beautifully nurtured family investment is out there on the road with him.

Then the rot sets in. Taxi runs are only on offer if the independent use of the car is the reward. You find yourself asking for a lift or waiting in the wind to be picked up. Gradually, without you being aware of it, your vehicle has become 'the car'. Possessive pronouns in your favour no longer apply. The new driver believes 'the car' to be in the same category as 'the television', 'the microwave', 'the stereo' – even 'the shower'. It's a household facility which is available for everyone's use but operates best when being controlled by the person who needs and uses it most. It goes without saying that this would also be the person who has become, overnight, the best driver in the civilised world.

Turbulence tells me, either in tones of sarcastic patience, delivered while he strokes the ceiling with his eyes, or very loudly indeed, with one foot already in the vehicle, that it was grossly unfair to allow him to become a licensed driver if I wasn't planning to let him use my car. He seems to have completely forgotten that the idea of him becoming a licensed driver was never mine.

After years of trying to deal with my unseen enemies, Everyone Else's Parents, I was appalled to find they are still around. Driving home from a restaurant the other night in the Good Husband's vehicle, we found our driveway lined with six or seven late model sedans, all of them fitted with shiny new Ps. Everyone else's parents, it seems, let the kids have mum's car on Saturday nights.

Should we hide our car keys and tell Turbulence to get a job and start saving? Unfortunately, it's just another example of bureaucratic cruelty that children mostly become eligible for their licences in the same year as they sit for their final school examinations. Time out for driving lessons has been, of course, an essential exception to Turb's strict study-and-eat regime. But we can hardly expect him to find time for the sort of job which would finance the quality car THIS boy has in mind.

'How would you feel if I bought a bomb and it broke down on the freeway when I was driving Rash to cricket practice or Serenity to piano?' Turbulence asked reasonably.

I wanted to say there was no freeway between our house and the cricket nets. I wanted to say I wished he was still the little boy who had to save his pocket money for six months before he could afford a bike tyre. But I had been soothing my stress with a gin and tonic or two, and my other two children had to be picked up before six.

'Here. Take our car,' I said as I handed him our keys.

BITS 'N Pieces

'Mrs Storm?' said the voice. 'It's Glynnis Sprig from Treestump South Public School speaking. Your son has had an accident.'

It was about time. At least a week had passed since any of my children had been involved in a crisis. Now I felt as if war had been declared or the doctor had said he would have to operate. I had something official to worry about.

Mrs Sprig was wonderful. Her tone was calm and controlled. There was no inflection, no hint of panic. There were few details.

She knew she had to provide enough information to get me up there fast but sane and all in one piece. Unlike Rash himself.

It's interesting, isn't it, how hard adult Australians work to keep up appearances even in the face of distressing news? In emergencies we restrain ourselves and keep to formalities, hiding our real feelings and questions in brackets inside our thudding chests.

'What happened?' I asked. ('Will he live? Have you called the ambulance? Will he be crippled for life?')

'He fell in the toilet block,' said Mrs Sprig.

'Is he badly hurt?' I asked. ('Is he screaming? Is there much blood? Will I recognise him?')

'He has chipped a tooth,' said Mrs Sprig.

'Aah,' I say, as my heart rate adjusts itself. ('When you say "chipped" are we talking dentures? Crowns? Thousands of dollars worth of oral surgery? Lifetime ugliness?') 'Is he very upset?'

'Yes,' said Mrs Sprig. ('He's sobbing his heart out and his shirt is soaked with tears and you didn't give him a hanky today and nobody knows what to say because he looks so awful.')

'Can he go back to class or did you want me to come and get him?'

'I think he would like to go with you to the dentist,' said Mrs Sprig. ('For heaven's sake come and take him out of here before his bellowing terrifies all the kindergarten children and the principal has a stroke thinking about the litigation.')

'It's quite a big chip, then, is it?' I can't help but probe.

'Quite big,' said Mrs Sprig. 'We'll expect you shortly then, shall we?'

It was quite a big chip and it involved Rash's two front fangs. In fact a less experienced school secretary would have been quite truthful (but risking her job) if she had screamed down the phone: 'Mrs Storm, come quick. Your baby boy has smashed both his beautiful front teeth into thousands of smithereens!'

As I sat in the dentist's surgery, watching with amazement as they constructed two magnificent new teeth for Rash out of concrete resin and told him to his joy that in future he should be wary about eating apples, I wondered how many more bits and pieces of this child would break off or become faulty before he could be considered a finished product.

I mean, we try so hard. The teeth which now lay in fragments on the floor of the school toilet block had been nurtured on gallons of milk, and regularly protected with fluoride, sealants and terrifyingly expensive toothbrushes. We had already begun paying into a fund to finance the inevitable braces which would straighten them to perfection. All the effort was now wasted — even the mouth guard, I thought bitterly, which I had bought for him only the day before.

Rash's eyesight is now enhanced by glasses. His rashes are cosseted with cortisone, his face is a feast of fifteen plus. His breathing is assisted by anti-allergy sprays. When he plays soccer his shins are protected with pads. At cricket his vital organs are hidden behind Hector. At school his feet grow healthily in proper leather shoes which endanger my bank book and his reputation.

It's sadly ironic that our first son, Turbulence, has remained wonderfully intact. The boy who hated school and would have loved to stay home with his Lego, rarely even had a runny nose. The only exception was the occasion when he broke his arm while he was watching his father dig a hole.

But Rash loves school and feels responsible for being there not only for the guys, who need him for handball, cricket, soccer and computer games, but for the teachers, whose vocations become relatively meaningless (he believes) without his presence in the classroom. It seems unfair that through illness and injury he loses weeks of school time, and frets desperately for some action.

Life's tough but Rash plays hard. He likes it that way.

I don't.

As we left the surgery and I ran a soothing hand over my cheque book, the dentist had some good news. From now on, Rash would need a mouth guard when playing sport. So there was one item I had paid for that wouldn't be wasted.

It's an ill wind.

DOUBLE Figures

Her eyes welled up, her lip went down, her face blazed red and tears lashed her cheeks. 'You realise you've ruined my life?' she screamed, flinging the sliver of fabric on the floor and sobbing as she ran from the room.

Actually, I'd asked Serenity if her new dress wasn't a bit short.

'Shouldn't you be studying?' I asked Turbulence, whose huge sneakered feet were hanging off the edge of the lounge, looking like part of the suite. He got up, scraped scornful eyes across the ceiling, and gave me a look of sheer incredulity. 'I don't know why you WORRY so much,' growled the drama prince, the anxiety kid, the boy to whom worry was once as integral as socks are to drawers. He slumped out the back door, a picture of disgust in checked flannel.

It had finally happened. Turbulence had nothing more to say to me. Nothing at all.

And he didn't even seem worried about it.

There are hormones all over our house. You can't see them but you know they're there — spilling into tears, oozing from pores, whipping up tempers, wreaking havoc in our home and multiplying every minute.

In those first heady days of parenthood, when you seriously believe that when the baby sleeps through the night your troubles will be over, puberty is simply not a consideration. Adolescence is as unfamiliar as a Pearl Jam CD playing at a dinner party.

But it creeps up quickly. The years fly by. One minute you're unpacking your bag from the maternity ward and the next minute the kids want to borrow your car.

Incredibly, I spent my first twelve years as a parent looking forward to my children's adolescence. I envisaged sleeping all night long in my own bed, cooking interesting food instead of mashing vegies for tiny palates, having offspring who had become organised and independent enough to run their lives efficiently on their own.

I thought I'd do better as the mother of teenagers. It's embarrassing to admit it, but I rather enjoyed my own adolescence and I wanted my kids to do the same.

I loved wearing big petticoats, pale lippy and tight T-shirts — of course it goes without saying that in those days my back didn't have any bulgy bits to match the ones on my front — I loved the Beatles, feared the Stones and adored the dances. My parents were not a blight on my life — my mother stayed up late at night shortening my minis; my father picked me up from the town hall disco and refrained from comment as my friends and I squashed into the back seat and squealed about boys all the way home.

Admittedly I must have slept in during the dawning of the Age of Aquarius and I was obviously on holidays or something when the free love was around — but what you don't have you don't miss.

Actually I thought I would do even better than my own parents, as unlike them I had read all the right books and listened to the experts. When puberty popped out of our children's pores, I had planned to be big on self-esteem and generous with praise; I would enjoy the new music, admire the new fashions and tolerate their dynamic new ideas.

What tripped me up initially was the fact that I wasn't prepared for a double dose!

We thought we'd been so clever. First we had a boy and then two years later, a little girl. The timing was wonderful — we only ever had one child at a time in nappies, Turbulence grew out of his cot and then his car seat just in time for his sister to use them and the high chair was vacated, scraped clean of crusted Weet-Bix and restored just in time for Serenity.

What we failed to take into account was that as girls mature about two years ahead of boys, Turbulence and Serenity would hit puberty within about five minutes of each other.

So no longer do we have to navigate our way around coloured crates of plastic toys in the kitchen, skates in the hall or boats in the bath. No more do we stagger from our cosy beds to nightmares and nocturnal accidents.

Instead we live with open pores, evil blackheads and half-squeezed tubes of pimple cream. We trip over tools and bits of bike and car chassis; our ears ache from the tuneless, grinding roar of two ghetto blasters which by agreement are never tuned to the same station. On the vanity bench in the bathroom, mere soap fights for a place among cans of hair spray, gap-toothed brushes, mousse, dental floss, cotton buds, skin cleanser, blemish sticks, deodorant sprays and shaving cream.

There are razor blades in the shower and sneakers the size of sofas lying in the hall. A large tube of anti-acne lotion is lolling in the hand basin along with a plastic dental plate which should be keeping someone's teeth straight. As the children's braces came at a cost equal to a quarter of my annual income, I wish they wouldn't allow their orthodontic appliances an RDO.

Moods swing, hormones ooze from every orifice, heads toss, shoulders shrug, eyes roll, tears fall, voices rumble, shriek and break. And that's when they're happy!

I finally said it yesterday. I couldn't believe that the words I swore would never leave my lips were being gathered by my rebellious brain to fling at my children.

'In MY day . . .' I said.

At night, as I stumble from my bed to find the source of some depraved hard metal band left squawking on top of a desk which has not held an open book for months, stopping off to demand that a sobbing heap beneath a doona postpone the noisy anguish of her friend's latest betrayal until daylight, I wonder when my tolerance and wisdom began to crumble.

As I demand information from my seventeen-year-old son, who stands in the 'let me escape' position (head and shoulders slumped in boredom, hands in pockets, eyes on the ceiling, mouth sneering, right foot pointing away in the direction of freedom, and spiky head nodding rhythmically to an unfamiliar beat) I can't help longing for the sensitive boy who has always driven me mad with his anxious questions and his desire to share with me his every emotion.

When Serenity leaves for the youth group disco in ragged jeans with holes in the knees and a T-shirt too big for her father, I can't keep my eyes from straying to the picture on the piano where the little white collar and the tartan dress remind me that not very long ago she was a Good and Sensible girl who never argued and rarely demanded any attention at all.

How can you live peacefully with two strange young people who seem to have undergone personality transplants without asking your permission; whose feelings swing from maudlin to manipulative, from ghastly to giggly, from loud and high to silently low; who bellow and roar one minute and then speak so quietly and so badly that you are constantly begging their pardon, as though you've done something wrong?

Well you can't. Live peacefully, that is. All you can do is make the most of their summer moods, those rare hours — well, minutes — when the world is revolving the right way for them, so that their smiles are sunny, their affections are warm and their hearts are happy.

In the meantime you just keep trying, even when they won't. You just keep talking, even when they don't; even when you'd like to be the one who slams the door, fires scathing salvoes of sarcasm, makes dramatic exits and sobs on the bed.

There are days when it's impossible.

So I screamed some scathing sarcasm, whirled dramatically up the stairs, slammed my door and collapsed into tears on my bed.

Nobody noticed.

After a while I washed my face and went to Serenity's room.

'I don't hate your dress,' I said to the soggy heap on the bed. 'Only somebody with lovely long legs like yours could wear a dress that short to a formal.'

Two arms appeared and wound around my neck.

'Can I go with Slender Harris and her big brother to the post-formal party afterwards?'

'No.' Silence. 'I don't know Slender, or her brother or her parents,' I said. 'You don't even know where they live.' Silence. Her arms began to slide away.

I took a deep breath and gritted my teeth. 'But if you like, your friends can come here for a little party first.'

Her arms tightened. 'I love you, Mum,' she whispered.

When I got back to the kitchen my son was back. 'Gotta eat early,' he said to his belt buckle. At least, I think that's what he said. 'Me 'n Mick are going to a movie.'

'Mick and I,' I murmured.

'Naah,' he rumbled. 'You're not invited.'

I took another deep breath and tried harder. 'I'm cooking your favourite dinner,' I said. 'Supermarket rissoles. If you're home by eleven and you don't plan to drink, you can borrow the car.'

For a fleeting second I saw his multi-thousand dollar teeth. 'You're cool, Mum,' he said clearly. 'Don't worry. You'd have to be a Richard Cranium to drink and drive. I won't be late because I'm going to hit the books tomorrow.'

He loomed over me and briefly something rough and stubbly brushed against my face. For a fleeting second I flinched; I clung to the memory of that small satin cheek, so regularly damp with tears, which used to tear my heart apart with love and pain and the whole damn thing.

I hugged him hard and rubbed out my tears on his flannel front. There was no going back. They were growing up and if I was going to enjoy life after children, I would have to forgive them for it.

Then cruel fate shoved twelve-year-old Rash into the room. 'Mum,' he said anxiously, 'I've got the hairiest legs of anybody in my class.'

They tell me that when they finally pulled me off the unfortunate child I was trying to get a nappy on him.

AND IN CONCLUSION...
there isn't one

After three children, twenty sleepless years, chronic anxiety, a stretched and soggy pelvic floor, the total disintegration of my self-esteem – and more love and laughter than I ever thought possible – I have to concede that there are no rules to parenting at all.

The inescapable fact is that once you lug your first nappy bucket through the laundry door, advice and theories slop over the tiles and go mouldy in the grouting.

Parenting is, after all, merely a service industry, a spectator sport. Children are born, not made, and twenty years will have to spin by before we find out whether our part in their development has been successful – by which time it will be far too late for us to do anything about it.

All we can do in the meantime is love our girls and boys like mad, hug them heaps, talk and talk to them, no matter what they say or do, build boundaries for them to bounce against, make the most of the good times, be there for them every minute that we can and always have a wet washer handy.

It's all trial and error, really, and occasionally we even learn from our mistakes.

But not often.